especially for

....

from

....

date

....

3-MINUTE DEVOTIONS

FOR A
Cat Lover's Heart

180 *Purr-fect* Readings

BARBOUR BOOKS
An Imprint of Barbour Publishing, Inc.

© 2016 by Barbour Publishing, Inc.

Print ISBN 978-1-63409-775-8

eBook Editions:
Adobe Digital Edition (.epub) 978-1-63409-876-2
Kindle and MobiPocket Edition (.prc) 978-1-63409-877-9

Published by Barbour Books, an imprint of Barbour Publishing, Inc., P.O. Box 719, Uhrichsville, Ohio 44683, www.barbourbooks.com

Our mission is to publish and distribute inspirational products offering exceptional value and biblical encouragement to the masses.

Member of the
Evangelical Christian
Publishers Association

Printed in the United States of America.

Introduction

Welcome to *3-Minute Devotions for a
Cat Lover's Heart*—a book just for cat lovers!
Here you'll find 180 devotional readings
celebrating faith, fun, and feline friends, as well
as God's love, voice, security, strength, friendship—
and more! Ideal for cat enthusiasts of all ages,
these devotions promise bountiful blessings.
It's a perfect way to start or end a day, or for a quick
pick-me-up in between, all the while helping you
grow closer to God and experiencing His
joy through the antics of our furry friends!

Examples of Patience

But thou, O man of God, flee these things; and follow after righteousness, godliness, faith, love, patience, meekness. Fight the good fight of faith, lay hold on eternal life, whereunto thou art also called, and hast professed a good profession before many witnesses.

1 TIMOTHY 6:11–12 KJV

Our kittens love their home in the barn. They are safe and well fed. They would contentedly stay there at all times, but they have a little admirer who lives in our house. She only has to approach one of her siblings with all the charm a two-year-old can muster and announce, "I want a little baby kitty." They succumb easily to her will, and the kitten is promptly produced.

The kittens have discovered that our house is definitely worth entering. There are warm, soft places to curl up. There's plenty of milk and a bit of meat. It couldn't get much better. But there *is* that little girl—the one who insists on carrying them everywhere in the crook of her arm, wrapping them in blankets and over-loving them. The house is a pretty great place if they can patiently endure the trials.

We face plenty of trials in this life. God asks only that we endure them faithfully and patiently. They are only for a season, and the heavenly reward that is to come is worth far more than any tribulation He asks us to endure on earth.

Father, I will patiently press on, looking forward to eternal life that lies ahead.

Great Escape

*"Can a woman forget her nursing child,
and not have compassion on the son of her womb?
Surely they may forget, yet I will not forget you."*

ISAIAH 49:15 NKJV

"Judy's cat has kittens. Can we have one? Please?" I begged my parents. Of course, I made the standard promises to care for it. Mom and Dad eventually agreed, and we selected a puff of fur from the litter. We named him Butterscotch for his golden color.

My folks, both raised on farms, insisted that Butterscotch should sleep in the basement. The first night he howled awhile, but soon quieted. In the morning I rushed to get him, but he was nowhere to be found.

"Momma! Butterscotch is gone!"

We'd barely started to search when Judy's mother called. "Are you missing a kitten? He's back on our porch."

I hurried over to retrieve him while Dad tried to discover how he escaped.

After two more nights of disappearances, Dad waited on the basement steps to spy on our kitten. When the house was dark, Dad heard a meow from outside and Butterscotch mewed in response. Dad watched him scramble up some boxes stacked near a window and Butterscotch's determined mother slipped her head through a tight space we hadn't noticed. She grasped Butterscotch in her mouth and wriggled him through the gap.

Dad patched the hole and agreed that Butterscotch deserved a warm bed—upstairs.

You never forget Your children, Lord. You rescue me,
no matter where I am. Thank You!

Let the Son Shine

But if we live in the light, as God does,
we share in life with each other. And the blood
of his Son Jesus washes all our sins away.

1 JOHN 1:7 CEV

After several dreary, cold, overcast days, Gretchen opened her bedroom blinds to bright sunshine. *It's about time we had some sunshine,* she thought to herself. Her big tomcat, Malcom, rubbed against her leg and then moved toward the door that led to the sunroom. "Oh, you want to go out and enjoy the sun?" she asked him. She opened the door and let him out. "I'll be right back," she told him. She walked to the kitchen for her first cup of coffee.

She hummed a little song as she poured cream into her cup. She could tell the sunshine was definitely lifting her spirits—she had noticed over the years that days of rain dampened her mood. She took her coffee to the sunroom to join Malcolm.

He didn't move a muscle as she entered the room. He lay on his side in full stretch as if to take up as much of the sun's warmth as he could soak in. Gretchen sat down and leaned her head back, following Malcom's example.

Lord, You are my light and my salvation. Just as I need sunshine,
I need Your love and light to shine on me.
Today I take time to soak in Your presence.
Infuse me with Your strength today.

Familial, Not Feral

See what great love the Father has lavished on us,
that we should be called children of God!

1 JOHN 3:1 NIV

When we lived on sixteen acres in rural Colorado, we had a big,
fluffy cat adopt us. My husband named her the most unoriginal
name possible, Whitey. Technically, she should have been called
Off-Whitey or Creamy, but my husband doesn't have artistic
tendencies. One time Whitey had kittens, but she hid them from us
in a shed on the property. For weeks, we'd only catch glimpses of
the kittens, until the day Whitey brought them to our house so we
could feed them.

It was a little tricky getting to know these feral kittens. But
one by one, they grew accustomed to us and let us pet them. The
friendliest one was pale, like her mother, so I called him Casper,
after Casper the Friendly Ghost. Whitey's behavior reminds me
of human behavior toward God. We take care of things on our
own—until things get too difficult. And then we come to Him out of
necessity even though God has desired our company all along.

Like Whitey brought her kittens to us, Jesus invites us
into God's family so the heavenly Father can love, care for, and
fellowship with us.

Thank You, heavenly Father, for inviting me into
Your family in Jesus. Thank You for the many
blessings that come with being a child of God.

Cat Craziness

Beloved, do not avenge yourselves, but rather give place to wrath;
for it is written, "Vengeance is Mine, I will repay," says the Lord.
ROMANS 12:19 NKJV

I had just fed our cat, Bruce, and left the house, where my high-school-aged son, Dexter, and his youth leader, Kyle, were getting ready for youth group. I had only driven just a mile down the road and they were calling me already. I was worried that something was wrong when I heard Kyle blurt out, "Shelley! You won't believe this!" It was quickly evident that he was laboring to talk because he was trying not to laugh hysterically. "Bruce—(pause for erupting laughter)—is peeing into the laundry—(gasping for air, more laughter)—and it is shooting through the laundry basket straight—(hah. . .gasp gasp)—into the dogs' water bowl!"

The scene was too hilarious to keep to themselves, and I was glad they called. I laughed all the way to my evening event.

While we joked later that Bruce was getting even with the dogs for something, he clearly was just marking his territory, and it was nothing some vinegar in the wash and a cleaned-out water bowl couldn't fix. The funny story did make me think about vengeance. What a relief it is that we can let God take care of it, even when we may feel like taking getting even into our own hands.

Lord, thank You for having my back. Help me
trust You today with any thoughts of getting even.
You are so faithful and know what is best.

This Little Light of Mine

Arise, shine; for thy light is come,
and the glory of the LORD is risen upon thee.
ISAIAH 60:1 KJV

Light. Bright. Brighter. Dark.

  Light. Bright. Brighter. Dark.

The rhythmic blinking light pulled me from a pleasant dream. Groaning, I pulled the sheet over my head.

  Light. Bright. Brighter. Dark.

I opened one bleary eye and peeked from under the cover.

My tuxedo cat, Squeakette, perched on the end table, tapping her nose against the touch lamp like a chicken pecking for worms. Her internal clock, responding to an empty tummy and the rising sun, proclaimed it was time for breakfast. At the end of each sequence, she paused to look at me. When I didn't respond, she repeated the tapping drill.

  Light. Bright. Brighter. Dark.

I yawned, threw back the covers, and sat up. "Hungry, little girl?"

Squeakette combined a purr with a mew, creating an endearing *chirrup* as her reply.

Assured I was awake with both feet on the floor, she hopped down and padded toward the kitchen to wait by her bowl. She had successfully coaxed me out of bed with her brilliant use of a lamp.

Squeakette's "wake up Mom" technique reminded me about my responsibility to share Jesus, the true Light, with others. I want God's light to shine steadily and persistently through me, coaxing those around me to awaken to His eternal love.

O Lord my God, I pray that I can show others Your Light that will one day dispel the darkness of night in our physical world forever. May they come to know and love You deeply!

Free Kitten?—NOT!

In him we have redemption through his blood,
the forgiveness of sins, in accordance with the riches of God's grace.
EPHESIANS 1:7 NIV

Mark wanted a good mouser for his barn. He saw the sign: "FREE KITTENS." He picked out the cutest puffball of the litter—a tawny kitten with white markings, including a white C on his back. During the less-than-three-mile trip home, however, the kitten got out of the box. He latched onto Mark's ankle with razor-sharp claws and teeth.

Startled, Mark yanked the steering wheel right. Truck, kitten, and driver plunged into the water-filled roadside drainage ditch. Thankfully, the truck remained upright. After a $125 tow out of the ditch, Mark and his "free" kitten arrived safely home.

Although God's gift of salvation is free to us, it cost our Savior everything. We have only to receive God's grace through faith in Christ's death for us. "For it is by grace you have been saved, through faith—and this is not from yourselves," we're told. "It is the gift of God" (Ephesians 2:8).

By week's end, between the vet visit and truck repair, Mark's "free" kitten, Crash, cost him over four hundred dollars. But no bill will come from our heavenly Father for our free gift of salvation. And it never will.

Father, thank You for the gift of salvation.
Help me to live in thankful obedience to You all my days.
In the name of the Savior who died for me. Amen.

The Good Samaritan Cat Rescue

Cheerfully share your home with those
who need a meal or a place to stay.

1 PETER 4:9 NLT

"Hey Dad," my daughter called. "Do you hear that?"

I concentrated on finding that wisp of a place lodged between what you actually hear and what you only imagine. I finally heard a mewing. My daughter and I trudged through the snow to a window near her room. There, matted with snow, was Sassy.

Her body shook under the matted fur and prominent snow unibrow.

A can of tuna and a little milk revived her as she recuperated in the sunroom.

She's not our cat, so caring for her wasn't our responsibility, but I couldn't help thinking about Jesus' story of the Good Samaritan as I worked to bring the ragged cat to safety.

My kids learned a lesson from our family rescue. I did, too. As my children helped me dig out the driveway, Sassy would venture from the sunroom and mew her approval. Then a tractor came down our street, backed into our driveway, and removed the seventeen inches of snow, saving us hours of work. We needed help, and someone we didn't know dropped by. There was something familiar about that.

Dear God, thank You for allowing my family to see the
joy in being Good Samaritans and the joy in receiving
the kindness of strangers. Thanks for adopted cats
and for adopting us into Your family. Amen.

Running Home

*"Serve Him with a loyal heart and with a willing mind;
for the L*ORD *searches all hearts and understands
all the intent of the thoughts."*

1 CHRONICLES 28:9 NKJV

Jak is a loud, affectionate cat. When you respond to his cries (which are difficult to ignore) and pick him up, he will usually knead on your neck, lick your face, or nuzzle into your hair. He also is eager to come when he's called.

One day after Jak had returned from a five-day hiatus in Ohio farm country, I was overjoyed to see he was all right. Feeling especially protective of him, I saw him get near the road and called out to him. He jerked his head in my direction and tore off running across our large open front yard. I held open the door and he ran straight into the house.

I started thinking about how well I hear God and if I go running straight to Him when I hear His call. It was humbling and challenging to realize how I long to be as responsive as Jak.

God, give me ears to hear You and a heart to follow You today.
I need You, God, in even the smallest of life's moments.

15

Recognize When It's Time to Rest

*"Be still, and know that I am God! I will be honored by
every nation. I will be honored throughout the world."*

PSALM 46:10 NLT

Daniel pushed his reading glasses back up onto his face as he
looked down to read a text on his phone. He noticed his wife, Jan,
still going a hundred miles an hour. "Babe, come and sit down."

"I can't. I've got to get a few more things done," she called as
she darted toward the laundry room.

When she walked through the living room again, Daniel stood
up, blocking the walkway. "Look at Missy," he said, directing her
line of sight toward their furry family friend curled up on the love
seat. "She always makes time to rest. Any time is the right time for a
catnap in her book. You can't keep going at this rate. You've got to
learn to pace yourself."

"You're right. I can't get it all done in a day. Maybe I should
follow Missy's example. Every time she takes a nap, I should sit
down and put my feet up," she joked.

"I don't think that's a bad idea," Daniel replied. "You've got to
take time for yourself."

Father, I live in a performance-driven world. I feel
guilty sometimes when I take time for myself, and yet
You have prepared a rest for me. Help me to let go of
the things I should and trust completely in You.

Mittens the Memorial

And he spake unto the children of Israel, saying, When your
children shall ask their fathers in time to come, saying,
What mean these stones? then ye shall let your children know,
saying, Israel came over this Jordan on dry land.
JOSHUA 4:21–22 KJV

Somewhere among my Christmas tree ornaments is a stuffed green felt mitten. Peeking out the top is a tiny kitten. This ornament, along with two others, is symbolic of a night many years ago—the night my husband asked me to marry him.

That night we rescued a tiny frightened kitten. We named him Mittens. Sure, it's not the most unique name, and he wasn't even the first Mittens I'd ever had. But this Mittens had six toes on each paw, so it just seemed appropriate. The following Christmas, I bought the ornament, a tangible reminder of a very special night.

Throughout God's Word, we see Him calling on His people to remember. He established memorial feasts. He commanded the Israelites to set up stones as a reminder, and He even instituted the Lord's Supper all because He wants us to remember those wonderful things He has done for us. We are people who easily forget the blessings of God. We're prone to wander. He wants us to have a way to look back. To remember. To move forward for Him.

Lord, let me not forget the great things
You've done on my behalf.

Prodigal

*"And he arose and came to his father. But when he was still
a great way off, his father saw him and had compassion,
and ran and fell on his neck and kissed him."*

LUKE 15:20 NKJV

When I was little, cats were allowed to wander outside. One evening, Butterscotch, my long-haired yellow cat, didn't come home when I called him. Our family scoured the neighborhood and surrounding areas. After a week, my parents gently told me that Butterscotch must have encountered some unspeakable disaster. I cried myself to sleep several nights and prayed for God to bring him home.

A year passed. My tears eventually dried. Then one morning Mom saw a fluffy yellow kitty sitting on our fence. In disbelief, she went to the door and called, "Butterscotch?"

He pranced into the house, rubbed against Mom's leg with a happy purr, and stopped where his food dishes used to be. He looked up as if to ask, "Where's breakfast?"

He was a little scruffy, but we welcomed him home with open arms and a joyful celebration. We never asked for an explanation about where our prodigal had spent that year.

That's how the Lord treats us when we wander away from His tender care. He eagerly welcomes us home as soon as we realize how much we need Him. All He wants is our love.

Heavenly Father, help me understand that no matter how far
I've gone, Your arms are open. Your love will hold me close.

God's Perspective

The wicked flee though no one pursues,
but the righteous are as bold as a lion.
PROVERBS 28:1 NIV

As a fiction writer, I give a lot of thought to a character's name. The name has to match the personality, social status, and time period. In real life, a fashion model may be named Gertrude, or a ditch digger Anthony, but not in a contemporary novel.

My daughter's kitten, Mouser, didn't get her name because of her hunting abilities. My then three-year-old daughter named her that because she was gray, cute, and tiny, like a mouse. Though Mouser was never any good at keeping the mouse population down, she kept my daughter happy and entertained.

The Bible says the righteous are as bold as lions. I rarely feel as bold as a lion. That's why it's important to meditate on scripture. God sees us as we are in Christ, not how others or even we ourselves see us. Verses such as the following strengthen and encourage us: "This righteousness is given through faith in Jesus Christ to all who believe" (Romans 3:22).

"So in Christ Jesus you are all children of God through faith" (Galatians 3:26). "But now in Christ Jesus you who once were far away have been brought near by the blood of Christ" (Ephesians 2:13).

Father, thank You that You look at me through the lens of Your Son. You see me as forgiven, righteous, and accepted. Please change me from the inside out to become more like Jesus.

Let's Agree to Be Wise

*She watches over the affairs of her household
and does not eat the bread of idleness.*

PROVERBS 31:27 NIV

Kendra respects the ideal of the "Proverbs 31 woman"—the wise wife extolled by such beautiful verses in Proverbs for running her household well. "That's going to be me," Kendra told her fiancé, Sam, as they prepared for their upcoming wedding. "I'll try to be wise in everything, including helping to control our costs."

"I'll match you in that," Sam promised. The two decided to set up a household budget in advance of them moving in together upon their marriage. One particular area of concern was the increasing cost of cat food and veterinary care.

"Linus is my cat," Kendra said. "I have a thousand dollars saved. That should cover cat food, litter, and shots for the next year. I'll save a bit each month from my job, and I'd like to keep that fund separate from our other accounts—meaning we don't dip into it for anything but cat expenses."

Sam knew how much her beloved pet meant to Kendra, so he agreed. He asked for the same consideration for his favorite hobby, cycling. He said he'd fund his cycling-related expenses from his own pocket and not borrow from their common bank account to pay for them.

"It's a deal," Kendra said. The two of them shared a kiss over their agreement.

Lord, we thank You for times when we come together in loving accord. May we always try to find common ground.

The Little Things

"His master replied, 'Well done, good and faithful servant!
You have been faithful with a few things; I will put you in charge
of many things. Come and share your master's happiness!'"
MATTHEW 25:23 NIV

At first, Bridgett was reluctant to consider her daughter Carrie's persistent request for a kitten, but after several weeks, she decided it might be nice to have a pet in the house. After all, her parents didn't allow her to have any pets growing up.

Carrie proved herself a fine pet owner. Not once had Bridgett had to clean the litter box, feed, or water the little one that Carrie named Daisy. "Look, Mom," Carrie called. "Daisy never misses a thing," Carrie chirped as her kitten rolled a ball of yarn across the living room floor.

Bridget noticed Carrie was right. Daisy paid attention to the littlest of things that Bridgett and Carrie normally wouldn't have noticed. Her eyes were always wide open—curious about every little thing, from a leaf that blew in to a coin that fell from Carrie's pocket spinning on the floor.

Lord, I get so caught up in the big things in life that I can easily miss the little things in life. I don't want to miss a single blessing from You. Open my eyes to see more of the little things that make this life more meaningful!

Will Scratch for Food

Also to You, O Lord, belongs mercy;
for You render to each one according to his work.
PSALM 62:12 NKJV

Friends insisted training a cat couldn't be done. I determined to prove them wrong when my long-haired tabby, Feathers, chose my antique bed frame to sharpen her claws.

Her old worn-out scratching post had lost its appeal over the years. I bought a new one and set it in front of her with *"Ta-da"* fanfare.

Feathers gave it an indifferent once-over, then sauntered away. The new-carpet smell must've offended her. Dosing it with catnip piqued her interest, but only long enough for her to roll around in it. The allure of mahogany seemed too strong.

I resorted to bribery. I put her in front of the post and moved her paws up and down over the carpeted covering. She begrudgingly dug her claws into it. I gave her a treat and praised her. She clawed again. I gave her another treat and more praise.

A week later, I realized the annoying truth—Feathers had trained me to keep a bag of treats in the drawer to shower her with praise and kitty candy. I swallowed my pride, knowing the bed frame would survive.

Feathers taught me to consider my own efforts for the Lord. Do I work to please Him or to garner rewards?

O Lord, help me to be mindful of my expectations
of blessings when I do good works for You.
Help me to serve You with a sincere heart.

Safe Haven

*For you have been my refuge, a strong tower
against the foe. I long to dwell in your tent forever
and take refuge in the shelter of your wings.*

PSALM 61:3–4 NIV

Our cat, Jak, is quite sure he's a dog. When we put a dish down for the dogs to enjoy, Jak comes running, too. When we call the dogs in, Jak often comes as well. He begs for food. He has his own loud request to be let outside, and often the dogs will be sitting next to him waiting for the same. Jak is also very confident, cuddling up with the dogs like he's one of them, while our other cats are a bit more cautious about this activity.

One day as I sat writing on the couch, the entire zoo (less the hermit crabs) lay around me in an afternoon slumber. Jak got up and decided he wanted to be right up against Zoey, the eighty-pound shepherd. Zoey startled from her snoring sleep and snapped at Jak, who recoiled and darted over to me. He looked at me sadly and curled up nearly on my lap, stretching his paw to my arm with a *"Did you see that?"* look in his eyes.

It made me think how sometimes we just aren't sure where we fit in, but with our Master, we always have a place.

Lord, thank You for being my steady hope
and love in all of the uncertainty of today.

Stand by Me

"The LORD your God goes with you;
he will never leave you nor forsake you."

DEUTERONOMY 31:6 NIV

"Dogs have people and cats have staff." So reads a contemporary proverb, probably the opinion of a dog lover or a condescending canine. That's not the case with Minnie, a cat who demonstrates unwavering loyalty to her young charges.

Five-year-old Jayli never has to walk to the school bus stop alone. Minnie walks right alongside her. She not only walks with Jayli, but she makes sure Jayli gets on the bus. She doesn't return home until the school bus pulls away with Jayli onboard. At night, Minnie snuggles in with Jayli, too.

Minnie doesn't overlook Jayli's little sister either. Skylee doesn't go to school yet, so at naptime Minnie assumes her post beside Skylee until suppertime or snack time ends their afternoon siesta.

Our Savior never leaves our side either. In the fourth psalm David wrote, "In peace I will lie down and sleep, for you alone, LORD, make me dwell in safety" (Psalm 4:8). Deuteronomy 31:6 is restated in the New Testament, too. In Hebrews 13:5 God reminds us again, "Never will I leave you." We cannot see or touch Him, but God is beside us just like Minnie snuggling in with her "staff" at bedtime or naptime.

Heavenly Father, when I feel frightened and alone,
remind me again of Your promises. Help me to
trust You although I can't touch You. Amen.

Like a Lion

Whoever dwells in the shelter of the Most High will rest in the shadow of the Almighty. I will say of the Lord, "He is my refuge and my fortress, my God, in whom I trust." Surely he will save you from the fowler's snare and from the deadly pestilence.

PSALM 91:1–3 NIV

It was all over the news—the story of a family cat who tackled a dog before it could bite her child. The dog ran—though he was bigger than the cat, he knew the danger of a protective feline. That housecat turned into a lioness when her boy was in danger. In her mind, that child was her cub.

God's protection of His children is fierce. So fierce, as a matter of fact, that the enemy tucks tail and runs when He shows up. That's why it's so important to stay close to Him. Oh, we may get a few scratches, but God's desire is to rescue His children from harm.

That's why He sent Jesus—it was a rescue mission. He put Himself in harm's way for our benefit. That kind of love is powerful, and it will drive away darkness. Our job is to stay close to Him so His rescue is swift and efficient.

Dear Father, thank You for protecting me.
Remind me to stay close to You.

The Welcome Committee

A man who has friends must himself be friendly.

PROVERBS 18:24 NKJV

Three doors down on the other side of the alley was a home, and in that home were two children who had two cats, and those two cats were supposed to be loyal to the boy and the girl that fed them. Instead, they spent most of their time sunning themselves in our backyard.

When we opened a door, both cats came running just like dogs would. Sassy would launch herself into our arms, and Cali would twist herself around our legs and purr like a jackhammer.

My memories of these two are far and away more potent than those of any other cat I've owned. Often the boy and the girl from three doors down would come to our back gate to collect their cats. They would apologize and scold the sister cats, but the two furry creatures would escape as soon as the children went inside.

There are people like Sassy and Cali that tend to irritate us. They barge into our lives and never seem to know when to go home. But maybe they're just showing themselves friendly and waiting for us to return the favor. Sometimes those with the most patience make the best friends.

Dear God, You want me to be friendly, but sometimes
I hide, failing to recognize there are others around me
who need friends. Help me be patiently friendly and
show Your love to those without friends. Amen.

An Unacceptable Sacrifice

If thou doest well, shalt thou not be accepted?
and if thou doest not well, sin lieth at the door. And unto
thee shall be his desire, and thou shalt rule over him.

Her name was Cinders. She was nearly perfect as far as cats go. She had a beautiful light gray coat that was silver tipped. She had darker gray points and features that were indicative of Siamese heritage. We never knew the origin of that. Like most of our cats, she had come from the barn, and as far as we could tell, she was the only one with these markings.

Cinders was friendly enough. She liked attention, but she never demanded it, and she certainly earned her keep. She was welcome indoors, but she often ventured into the great outdoors as well. It was after one of her outings that she decided to bring me a gift.

I'm sure to her it seemed wonderful, but when I found the dead mole lying in my bedroom doorway, I was not pleased. My otherwise wonderful cat had not done well!

How often do we pridefully make an offering to God that isn't what He wants from us at all? He wants us to give Him our best. Giving anything less is sin lying in wait on our doorstep. When we offer a substitute gift because we aren't willing to sacrifice what God requires, we do not do well, and our sacrifice will be turned away!

Dear God, I offer that which You ask of me.

No More Blame Game

The integrity of the upright will guide them,
but the perversity of the unfaithful will destroy them.
PROVERBS 11:3 NKJV

Nina shut the bathroom door, leaving Phoebe, her small kitten, in the bathroom. She felt bad leaving her shut in throughout the night, but it was the only way she and her husband Rob could get any sleep. Phoebe's wild side came out at night.

Nina dozed off to sleep, but minutes later she was awake. Phoebe had escaped; the bathroom door stood open. "Rob, you left the bathroom door open! Phoebe's out!" she said, waking him. "What?" he whispered, half-awake. "No, I've been in bed. I didn't get up."

After Phoebe escaped a second time and Rob denied it again, Nina put her in the bathroom and waited. She heard a few thuds inside the bathroom, as if Phoebe was throwing herself against the door. Then, without help from anyone, the door opened, and Phoebe jumped down from the bathroom counter and walked back into the bedroom.

Nina couldn't believe it. The tiny kitten opened the door all by herself! She felt bad for blaming Rob for leaving the door open. She went out to the garage for the pet carrier. Then she put Phoebe to bed inside, shutting the door to the guest bedroom.

Lord, I'm guilty of jumping to conclusions. Help me to uncover all the facts and then respond with Your mercy in love to each situation rather than choosing to blame others.

Fred

Praise be to the God and Father of our Lord Jesus Christ,
the Father of compassion and the God of all comfort.
2 CORINTHIANS 1:3 NIV

Fred, a long-haired gray and white cat, started out as a stray, but despite our initial unwillingness, he wormed his way into our family. I soon became glad that Fred persisted. After a long day of homeschooling my kids, working at a daycare, and writing, I'd stretch out on the couch, and Fred would act as a cuddly hot-water bottle. I would stroke his luxurious fur as he sat on my chest and purred.

Romans 1 says that God's creation declares His glory and His invisible nature. When I read that scripture, I usually think of the majestic mountains, the mysterious oceans, the life-giving force of rivers. However, cats are His creation, too. A big gray ball of fluff bringing its comfort also declares God's qualities, because God comforts us (2 Corinthians 1:4).

We are not alone in this world. Jesus calls us friends (John 15:15). He wants us to abide in Him like a branch connected to its vine draws nourishment from it (John 15:5). He says where two or three gather in His name, He is in their midst (Matthew 18:20). The Holy Spirit lives right inside of us (1 Corinthians 6:19). We have an intimate, loving, comforting God. Perhaps since He can't be here in bodily form, He gave us cats like Fred.

Thank You, Lord, that You are with me and You care about me when I'm feeling down, blue, or plain exhausted.

I Beg Your Pawdon...

At noon Elijah began to taunt them. "Shout louder!" he said. "Surely he is a god!"... So they shouted louder and slashed themselves... until their blood flowed.... But there was no response, no one answered, no one paid attention.

1 KINGS 18:27–29 NIV

Have you seen the Facebook video clip?

A deaf man taught his cat how to communicate with him in sign language. As the man eats a snack, his cat watches him and then gently taps his arm with his front paw. When his owner looks at him, the cat taps his paw to his own mouth. The man holds a tidbit on his finger and his cat gets his share of the snack. If the cat wants more, he taps and points again. He never snatches any food from his master, nor does he scratch him or box his arm. He just gives him a gentle tapping reminder and signal.

The false prophets of Elijah's day tried everything to get the attention of their non-existent god. Elijah had no such problem when he called on the one the Bible calls "the only God" (Jude 25). "Answer me, LORD," was his simple request (1 Kings 18:37). And God did.

Sometimes even a spoken prayer is not necessary. *"Before they call I will answer,"* promises the one true God (Isaiah 65:24, emphasis added).

Mighty God, hear my heart's deepest cries in today's tough challenges. Amen.

Getting Our Attention

Let the heavens rejoice, let the earth be glad;
let the sea resound, and all that is in it.
Let the fields be jubilant, and everything in them;
let all the trees of the forest sing for joy.
PSALM 96:11–12 NIV

Ezra doesn't like people. He avoids them as much as possible. . . even Summer, his owner. He really just wants to be left alone.

That is, until Summer pays attention to someone else. The moment she gets on the phone, Ezra appears from wherever he was hiding and crawls all over her. "Meow, Meow. Meeeee-oooooo-eee-oooow." The more Summer tries to shush him, the more he sings and mews and hollers. He wants to make sure she understands his annoyance that she would dare speak to anyone other than him.

God is kind of like Ezra. Oh, He doesn't hide from us. But He tries desperately to get our attention. He wants, more than anything, for us to focus on Him. He whispers in the wind. He winks in the wildflowers. He shouts in the sunset. He is everywhere we look, begging for us to acknowledge Him. He adores us, and He wants us to love Him back.

Dear Father, thank You for loving me. Thank You for reminding me of Your presence in so many beautiful ways. Forgive me for taking my attention off of You. I want to be conscious of Your presence, every minute.

Magnificence

*For since the creation of the world His invisible attributes
are clearly seen, being understood by the things that
are made, even His eternal power and Godhead,
so that they are without excuse.*

ROMANS 1:20 NKJV

His beautiful striped head was the size of a beach ball. His yawn,
with his four-inch canine teeth, could grab a volleyball. He looked
over at me with curious eyes, and I wished I could play with him
like I do with my own cat. I would rub his belly until he grabbed my
hand with two paws, or playfully palm his head until he batted back
in fun. But I would likely die for that activity.

I love tigers, but God knew that wouldn't work out for me on
this side of the Fall. So, He gave me my manageable cats. I truly
see them as a gift. I get to enjoy playing with them and admire the
big wild cats for just what they are—each cat a display of God's
workmanship, His creative brilliance.

God, thank You for the beauty and magnificence
of Your creation. You show Yourself a
little bit more to me each day.

Divided Loyalties

And if it seem evil unto you to serve the LORD, choose you
this day whom ye will serve; whether the gods which your
fathers served that were on the other side of the flood,
or the gods of the Amorites, in whose land ye dwell:
but as for me and my house, we will serve the LORD.

JOSHUA 24:15 KJV

Growing up, it was a rare thing for me to be allowed to have a cat. When I married my wonderful farmer husband, all of that changed. I had plenty of cats for the asking. Some were made into pets, while others were enjoyed more at a distance. It didn't take the cats long to realize that if they visited our porch they would receive treats. Evidently they spread the word because soon our porch was inhabited by feline friends.

This is all well and good except that I am also a bird lover and have worked hard to attract birds to our yard. The cats are also bird lovers in their own way. One spring day, my children came running to inform me that one of the cats had killed a bluebird. I love the cats, but at that moment I did not. It came down to deciding which creature would get my loyalty.

Daily we make that decision on a spiritual level. Will God get our love, our all? Or will our loyalty be elsewhere? We cannot split our love. God gets all or none.

Lord, I choose You!

Super Cat

For he will order his angels to protect you wherever you go.
PSALM 91:11 NLT

Marcie's fifteen-year-old calico, Corky, was content to spend his days asleep in a patch of sunshine on the bedroom carpet. Marcie enjoyed retirement; she spent time with family and worked on volunteer projects. Marcie and Corky were totally satisfied with their tranquil arrangement.

One day, Marcie's married granddaughter called. "Grandma, can we stay with you a few days?"

"Sure! When are you coming?"

"In about fifteen minutes. We got to town yesterday, and it isn't working out at Brad's parents' house."

In spite of the short notice, Marcie was delighted to spend time with them, especially since their family included a one-year-old baby. What Marcie hadn't expected was a fifty-pound bulldog named Max and an exuberant kitten. The house was transformed from calm to chaos.

Instantly, Corky was duty-bound to protect his mistress. Every time Max wandered near Marcie, Corky stood beside her, hissing and scratching with his clawless front paws. Max was so startled that he retreated to a far corner. When the kitten wanted to get acquainted, Corky, empowered to take on the world, managed to frighten her away, too. He was a fully attentive guard.

The baby apparently confused Corky. Someone that size probably wasn't dangerous, so Corky avoided him.

As soon as the visitors left, the bedroom sunshine beckoned an exhausted Corky.

Lord, You are my true protector. Thank You for understanding my needs, always prepared to defend me in times of trouble. Thank You that You never grow weary!

My Little Prince

"I was sick, and you cared for me."
MATTHEW 25:36 NLT

Rufus thought I was punishing him when I put healing salve on his wound. He had tangled earlier that day with Carlito, another tom in our house. After his vet visit, Rufus was in no mood to be handled, even by me. He squirmed out of my arms and ran off to a far corner of the house to hide.

"Sweetness, where are you?" I got down on all fours trying to find out where he was. I finally located my little patient under the bed in the spare bedroom.

"Baby, I love you," I cooed. "Please come out." No luck; the trust factor between us was gone. I extended the broom handle as far as I could beneath the bed without touching him. He hissed, and I stopped. I didn't want to scare him further just to get him out for more meds, poor little guy.

"Alright, Rufus. You come to Mama when you want. I love you." I retreated and left him in peace. By dinnertime he was hungry enough to reappear. He gave me "the glare," letting me know I better not try anything. I set his food down and walked off. Later, he sauntered over to my computer station where I was surfing the net for sites on cat psychology.

"C'mere," I said, holding out my hand. "You're my little prince." We re-bonded. All was forgiven.

I praise you, Lord, for giving me wisdom in knowing how to care for my animal companions.

Familiar Footsteps

*"When he has brought out all his own, he goes on ahead of them,
and his sheep follow him because they know his voice. But they
will never follow a stranger; in fact, they will run away from him
because they do not recognize a stranger's voice."*

JOHN 10:4–5 NIV

Elsie and her owner, Hannah, live in an apartment complex where
people come and go all day, every day. Elsie pays them no mind
whatsoever. She's only interested in Hannah.

If Hannah leaves, Elsie is on high alert. And when Hannah
comes back, Elsie knows long before anyone else. She knows her
master's footsteps, and she waits by the door to greet her beloved
owner when she arrives. Even on noisy, busy days, Emma can
identify the sound of Hannah's feet approaching.

I want to be that way. I wish I could block out everything
but my Master. I long to be so familiar with His footsteps that I
recognize Him even in the midst of chaos. The more time I spend
with Him, the more tuned in I am with His presence. I want to stay
close to Him, and when it seems He's disappeared, I'll wait by the
door for His return.

Dear Father, thank You for being a good Master.
I want to know You more. I want to recognize You
in the middle of noise and chaos. Teach me to
recognize Your footsteps and to know Your voice.

Identifying Marks

I bear on my body the marks of Jesus.
GALATIANS 6:17 NIV

Stacey sports a string of paw prints up her left arm. Her tattoos identify her as a cat lover. Since her cat, Harley, has the colors of a black and orange motorcycle by the same name, she bought him a leather collar. Harley's fashionable biker collar was almost his demise.

While grooming one day, Harley's tongue got caught in his collar. He choked and gasped for air, but soon his tongue turned blue and he slumped to unconsciousness. Stacey sprang into action. She cut off the collar and began CPR on her now-lifeless cat. Thankfully, Harley started to rally. With some supplemental oxygen and additional care at the veterinarian's office, he made a full recovery. He's kept his name, but not the leather collar. Harley wears a breakaway plastic collar for identification now.

What identifying marks do you bear as a Christian? Some Christians, even today, have telltale marks on their bodies as a result of persecution, as Paul said he did. Whether or not we bear physical scars or marks or choose an identifying tattoo, all of us who are followers of Jesus should be identifiable as Christ's disciples by lifestyle. Like the early disciples, others "took note that these men had been with Jesus" (Acts 4:13).

Lord Jesus, I pray that in all my thoughts and conduct
I show a likeness to You. I want my life to bring
honor to You and Your holy name. Amen.

Comforted

*"Now therefore, do not be afraid; I will provide for you and your
little ones." And he comforted them and spoke kindly to them.*

GENESIS 50:21 NKJV

Our sage cat, Ed, was not atypical of the cat stereotype, hiding from
strangers and most people if he wanted quiet, which was most of
the time. But in a mysterious way he would occasionally show up
and be the comfort cat when he somehow sensed a need for comfort
was in order.

One night we had family friends over for dinner. They had
recently lost their college-aged daughter suddenly to a virus.
After we all ate, our school-aged kids went off to hang out in the
basement while we adults sat together. We passed long silences
just being present and willing to sit in the pain with them. These
were incredibly hard days to get through for their family. The father,
Bryan, sat looking out the window, limp on an overstuffed armchair.
Just then, Ed walked slowly into the room, slinked up the arm of the
chair to the chair back and curled gently around the back of Bryan's
neck like a fur collar. Ed looked at us then softly closed his eyes.
Bryan typically does not care for cats at all, but he sat there and
accepted the comfort.

Father, thank You for the extra comforts You
provide in unexpected ways. If You need me,
lead me today to be where I may be a comfort.

Daisy

*Who comforteth us in all our tribulation, that we may be
able to comfort them which are in any trouble, by the
comfort wherewith we ourselves are comforted of God.*

2 CORINTHIANS 1:4 KJV

The day my daughter brought Daisy home was a happy day. Daisy
was the sweetest, tiniest kitten, and we were happy to welcome her.
For a few days, all was complete joy. Daisy was loved and cared for
as if she were royalty.

Then one day we noticed that Daisy didn't look well. She
wouldn't eat or play, and it was very clear that her time with us was
limited. We did what we could, but we lost her anyway. My daughter
was devastated.

As a mother, my heart broke for my precious girl. Experiencing
a loss is never easy, and for a child who knows only life and joy and
expectation, this can be such a blow. Sometimes as a parent it can
be difficult to know how best to comfort a hurting child. Thankfully,
we have a perfect example in the comfort that Christ gives us.

It's in moments like these that we may come to understand
just a little bit about the trials God has allowed into our lives. They
might not make sense until we have the opportunity to be there for
someone who is facing a similar hurt, and we are reminded of the
depth of God's wisdom.

Let me be used by You to bring
comfort to one who is hurting.

Looking for Approval

I am not trying to please people. I want to please God.
Do you think I am trying to please people? If I were
doing that, I would not be a servant of Christ.

GALATIANS 1:10 CEV

"Papa, Lucy is a showoff," Randall said. Papa looked at his five-year-old grandson quizzically. "That cat wants you to clap for her and tell her what a good job she did bringing that old dead mouse up on the porch," Randall continued.

"That's her job," Papa replied.

"Yes, I guess," Randall laughed, "but she also brings old rags, strings, and other things to you that aren't her job. She will do anything to get you to pay attention to her."

"Yes," Papa nodded. "Most people like attention, too. We want to know that people approve of the things we do, but if you have Jesus in your heart, you don't need other people to clap for you and tell you how good you are. God is the person you want to please first. His approval is the most important, and you don't have to do anything to be loved by Him."

Jesus, thank You for Your unconditional love.
You accept me just the way I am. You forgive me
right in the middle of my mess. It has nothing to do with
what I've done and everything to do with what You've done.

God Welcomes Us

"For I will be merciful toward their iniquities,
and I will remember their sins no more."
HEBREWS 8:12 ESV

When Frisky had two kittens, my kids named them Geordi and Data after Star Trek characters. Data was a tiger kitty like her mama, but Geordi was unique—his black fluffy fur with large orange dots looked almost like a clown suit. We had recently moved from Colorado to Pennsylvania to be closer to my parents and lived just up the road from them. Dad had Alzheimer's and Mom had a lot of health problems, too.

Oddly enough, one good thing about Alzheimer's was that Dad forgot he hated cats. When I was growing up, if I ever brought cats into the house, he'd promptly kick both cats and kids out. However, I had freedom to take Geordi and Data into my parents' home. Dad enjoyed watching the two kittens tussle and chase each other all over the living room.

When we put faith in Jesus, God remembers our sins no more, meaning He doesn't bring them to mind. Like Dad welcomed Geordi and Data into his home, God welcomes us into His throne room. When we come to Him, we don't have to worry about Him evicting us. We can now come to Him boldly.

Father, thank You for sending Your Son to pay
for our sins. You forgive us, and You actually take
pleasure in our company. Thank You for Your love!

When Life Gets Crazy

"He refreshes my soul. He guides me along
the right paths for his name's sake."

PSALM 23:3 NIV

Things were getting crazy in my life, so I took the cat and curled up on the sofa and just sat there, reflecting on things. Or thinking about nothing, because my mind was in such a whirl that it just went blank. I had troubles at work and uncertainties in my relationships. It was all too much.

The sun was going down outside the window. A patch of orange sunlight on my apartment wall was the only light in the small room. That's all I needed to keep myself anchored. The world outside was quieting down for the night. Maybe things would look better in the morning. Until then, I had time to get things together in my own mind. Already they weren't looking as bad as they did an hour ago when I first got home.

"Chauncey," I said to my rescue cat, "am I doing the right thing? Oh, if only you could talk." So many decisions to make, but I wasn't alone. My dear animal friend was with me, and how it helped me to stroke his soft fur and hear him purring like everything was fine. That calmed me down and made me feel more at peace.

"Thank you, Chauncey," I told him. "You're helping me a lot."

Thank You, Lord, for providing quiet times of
refreshment for our souls. You are in control.

Cat Hero

God demonstrates his own love for us in this:
While we were still sinners, Christ died for us.
ROMANS 5:8 NIV

Late one summer night, I brought Mom a ragdoll cat named Panda, whose eyes were as blue as Mom's. When we let her out of the cage, she promptly hid in the garage. . . We gave up trying to coax her out.

The next day, it was 106 degrees. Mom searched and called Panda without success.

Worried, she called my brother Mike. He stopped over after work with a flashlight, determined to find Panda in the hot garage.

Finally, he spotted her in a box behind a bike. Panda scurried behind a fridge and disappeared. Undaunted and sweaty, Mike found her much later. Panda had squeezed through the cover of a dirty wooden car-jack box. He soothed her as he wiped all the dirt and spider webs off her fur. When he carried her into the cool house, she promptly fled behind the TV.

Panda remained skittish with everyone except Mom and her hero. Every time she saw Mike, she jumped on top of the recliner to sit and wait for him to pet her.

We have a hero, too. His name is Jesus. Some of us ran from Him, not realizing time was running out, but He never gave up. He sweat great drops of blood to save us from the darkness, and He delivered us from all our fears and put us in a safe place.

Thank You, Lord, for loving me.

Top Dog

Keep back thy servant also from presumptuous sins.
PSALM 19:13 KJV

Newlyweds Pam and Frank and their cat, Jasper, eagerly awaited the arrival of Pam's firstborn child. Well, Pam and Frank eagerly awaited the baby's arrival. Back then, women stayed in the hospital for a few or several days after giving birth, so when the time came, Jasper was alone a lot. Something he wasn't used to.

Once Pam and the baby were discharged, Frank brought them home. Jasper was not happy with the new family addition. He eyed Doug suspiciously; he ignored Pam. Then he became destructive. Feline teeth marks began showing up on objects throughout the house. Jasper never adapted to the interloper's presence. One day, he stuck his tail up in the air, went off, and found himself another home nearby.

Apparently Jasper presumed he would always be the "top dog" in the household. Sometimes I take that "my way or no way" attitude with God. He doesn't answer my prayers as quickly as I *need* them answered. Or He doesn't answer them how I *want* them answered. So I sulk and pout and cry and wait for the Lord to give into my demands. Guess what? He never does.

"Our God is in heaven; he does whatever pleases him" (Psalm 115:3 NIV). Whatever pleases Him is good because He is good. I need to confess my presumption and humbly submit to Him.

God, forgive me for my stubbornness;
give me a submissive heart.

The Kitten-Napper

And he said unto them, Take heed, and beware
of covetousness: for a man's life consisteth not in
the abundance of the things which he possesseth.

LUKE 12:15 KJV

This is the story of two mama cats. One was named Lovely and the other named Truckfree. Lovely was, as the name implies, a healthy, reasonably attractive cat who gave birth to a litter of fine kittens.

Truckfree was a rather plain and obviously more timid cat. I say "obviously" because we were never able to hold her long enough to realize that she was female. (Hence the name Truckfree—well, that, and the fact that a small child named her.)

One day, much to our surprise, Truckfree also gave birth to a litter of kittens. That's when she became "Lizzy." So Lizzy had kittens, but they were small, and she wasn't exactly motherly, so we lost them.

Soon we noticed that a couple of Lovely's kittens were missing. They were too young to wander far by themselves, and Lovely didn't seem to be moving them. After some investigation, we found them, but they continued to disappear. Soon we discovered the culprit—it seems Lizzy wanted the kittens for herself.

Lizzy's envy caused no small stir in our family. She wasn't caring for the kittens, just stealing them. Envy causes great grief for cats and humans alike. That's why God calls covetousness a sin. He knows what's best for His children, and when we overstep His plans longing for something "better," it only causes problems.

Lord, help me be content with
what You know is best for me.

The Professor

*From the end of the earth will I cry unto thee, when my heart
is overwhelmed: lead me to the rock that is higher than I.*

PSALM 61:2 KJV

The Professor is a hefty Maine coon cat who lives two doors down. He likes to wander the neighborhood at night. When our miniature rat terriers go out for their early morning stretch, they often find the Professor perched on the eave of our tool shed, about four feet off the ground. Despite the frequent ritual of jumping, barking, growling, and leaping, our tiny dogs have never managed to reach the Professor. Each time they come close to his position, the cat backs up the roof a scant inch. The frantic efforts of the dogs seem to amuse him. Perhaps he has learned something that our dear dogs have not—the advantage is always with the party on higher ground.

It is also advantageous to walk on God's "higher ground" in our lives. God spoke through the prophet Isaiah concerning the way in which His people should conduct themselves. In chapter 55, God says, "As the heavens are higher than the earth, so are my ways higher than your ways and my thoughts than your thoughts" (Isaiah 55:9 NIV). For those who forsake their wickedness and turn to His path, He promises an everlasting covenant of love. He offers food to the hungry and water to the thirsty. His higher ways are a place of refuge and blessing.

Dear Jesus, I rejoice today in Your everlasting love.
Lead me in Your higher way.

He Loved Me First

We love because He first loved us.
1 JOHN 4:19 NIV

Sue wasn't a cat person. She didn't want a cat. She didn't like cats. Never had, and she never planned to. Then along came Buck. He showed up one day and decided he was home. Not only that, but he decided Sue was his best friend.

She'd sit on the porch. He'd jump in her lap. She'd shoo him away. He'd lay at her feet. The more she resisted him, the more he loved her.

Isn't that how God loves us? He reaches out to us, and we push Him away. Yet He never gives up. He just keeps coming back and back and back, offering His presence, His love, His affection. And He forgives us for all those times we reject Him. He wants, more than anything, to have a relationship with us, and He'll stop at nothing to get it.

Eventually, Sue gave in and decided she might like Buck a little bit. From that moment, they were the best of friends. God waits for each of us to decide we love Him. When we do, we can know He will be our best friend for all of eternity.

Dear Father, thank You for loving me first. Forgive me for pushing You away. I want to be close to You, to live in Your presence and enjoy Your friendship. I love You.

Be Careful, Not "Dareful"

Carefully follow the terms of this covenant,
so that you may prosper in everything you do.
DEUTERONOMY 29:9 NIV

The ancient Israelites were instructed to "follow the rules" so that things would go well for them in life. It's good advice for us today, too. Rules and regulations are there for a reason. God's guidebook is a helpful and holy road map for life.

Cats instinctively understand that their owners set the rules in the household. Much is said about the independent nature of cats, but many owners comment on how their cat picks up fast what is permitted and what is not.

For instance, Smokey is an adventurous, inquisitive cat who lives with his human family in a large old house. He likes to explore, but even he knows that there are places where his humans don't want him to go.

The trapdoor to the old cellar is always kept closed. His humans won't let him go down there. To protect him, they entice him into the kitchen with food, then close the glass doors to keep him locked in that small space. That's when Mother does her laundry. She lifts up the rug and pulls up the creaky trapdoor. Unbeknownst to her, Smokey followed her down there once. What joy, searching the dark corners for mice! But he got trapped in the cellar for hours when Mother went back upstairs. The cat learned his lesson. No more being the escape artist for Smokey.

Lord, help me always remember, trust and obey.

A Small Zoo

"Let's go." He motioned with his head as he sat waiting at the top of the steps. "Soon," he said with his eyes.

Our house contains a small zoo composed of four cats, a dog, and two hermit crabs. To keep the dog from eating the cat food, their dish is in the basement on a shelf. If he must eat in the dungeon, Bruce prefers to have company for dinner. So he waits and begs for one of us to accompany him downstairs for a few minutes. It's sweet. Each time I walk down, he nearly dances around my feet then runs ahead to his bowl, "See, here it is! Can you put more in here? It makes me nervous when it's half empty." This is what his face tells me every time.

This reminds me how often I need company, too. Furthermore, when I have to walk into some dark places in the heart work of life, I could use a companion. Sometimes it's only Jesus, and sometimes He gives me a friend.

Lord, show me today where You need to shine into
the darkness, even if it's within my own heart.

Patience Perfected

So let it grow, for when your endurance is fully developed,
you will be perfect and complete, needing nothing.

JAMES 1:4 NLT

Digging through a box of old pictures, Autumn stopped as her eyes fell to a picture more than twenty years old. It was a picture of her now twenty-three-year-old son as a toddler, asleep on the couch with his head resting on their cat Jesse's stomach. Autumn smiled, remembering Jesse's patience with Caleb.

Jesse, a small ball of fur when they got him, adjusted well to a new baby in the house. They grew up together those first few years. Jesse teased Caleb with his tail as he was learning to crawl and endured the moments Caleb picked him up as a toddler and carried him here and there. Jesse never complained, even though his face said, "Help me, pleeee-ase!"

Autumn instantly thought of Jesse's perfect patience and endurance each time she lost her own with Caleb. When he spilled the milk for the third time in an evening, fell across the living room floor—causing all the clothes she'd folded to unfold—or when he deliberately disobeyed and couldn't seem to stay in the timeout chair, Jesse would look at her with understanding. "Good ol' Jesse," she said. "Thanks for those many reminders."

Heavenly Father, patience often seems out of my grasp. Help me to hold onto patience. I choose to let patience have her perfect work in me today!

Enter into God's Rest

There remaineth therefore a rest to the people of God.
HEBREWS 4:9 KJV

At any given time, we can look around us and find one or more cats curled up asleep. Our kitten, Ash, who is the one most often invited into the house, has a favorite place he likes to nap. He seems to feel safest atop the couch and behind the curtain. It doesn't hurt that this is where the warm sunlight is at its best. That spot is an open invitation to him. It says, "Come. Relax and enjoy the peace and safety you'll find here."

We have an invitation like that from our heavenly Father. The trials and temptations of this world try to choke us, but God opens His arms to us and says, "Come. Rest. Be at peace."

He's made this offer to all, but many reject His love. They choose to limp through life, staggering as they try to do it on their own.

Yet God continues to offer. "I gave my Son for you. Trust Him. Let Him take on your sin and despair. Accept the rest and peace that He wants to freely give you!" Many refuse to believe. Many choose not to trust Him. Oh, what a sad, desolate life that rejects Jesus day by day! Don't be one who turns from this offer. Accept this rest in Christ. Be refreshed in the salvation that He offers.

In Your mercy You died that we might find rest.
Oh that we all would trust You today!

Hidden Treasure

*"I will give you hidden treasures, riches stored in
secret places, so that you may know that I am the Lord,
the God of Israel, who summons you by name."*

ISAIAH 45:3 NIV

Our friend's cat, Ralph, stayed home when the family left town, and I was often the designated cat sitter. He liked me, and I enjoyed getting my kitty fix at their house.

One day I couldn't find him. The family kept most rooms closed, so his space was limited. Usually when I called his name, Ralph trotted out for some playtime and treats. But that day, I called and called. I searched every possible cubbyhole and was beginning to panic when he still didn't turn up. Had he slipped out the door when I came in? It didn't seem possible.

Their neighbor was feeding him on alternate days, so I called them. "Is Ralph by any chance at your house? I can't find him anywhere."

"No, he was there yesterday."

As I continued to hunt, I heard a rustle coming from a dresser drawer that was slightly ajar. No meows, just a tiny sound. I slid the drawer open carefully. There sat Ralph, in a nest of jewelry and scarves, including a feathery boa. He reminded me of a king overseeing his realm. He blinked, stretched, and hopped out to claim some people time.

Dear Lord, teach me never to hide from You
or hoard earthly treasures but to rejoice
in the riches of my relationship with You.

Nestled in His Love

"Let the beloved of the LORD rest secure in him,
for he shields him all day long, and the one
the LORD loves rests between his shoulders."

DEUTERONOMY 33:12 NIV

When we first got our calico cat, Snickers, she'd climb up on the back of my neck and fall asleep. To the tune of praise music and a kitten's purr, I sought the Lord. Those were some of my favorite prayer times, being comforted not only by the Holy Spirit but also by an adorable kitty.

Sometimes, I feel like a kitten resting on God's shoulders. My soul purrs as His Spirit strokes me with His love. I take comfort in His presence, trusting that He loves me, protects me, and provides all I need.

From the creation of Adam and Eve to the establishing of Israel to the sending of His Son, God's desire has always been to dwell with His people. He made humans for Him to love and to be loved by them. Sin separates us from Him, so He sent Jesus. The greatest thing about redemption is that, in Christ, we are in fellowship with God. Let us not neglect the opportunities we have to simply cozy up in His love like a kitty cuddling her human.

Father, thank You for sending Jesus that we might fellowship with You. Lord, I draw near, trusting You are drawing closer to me.

Over the River and Beyond

" 'He was lost, but now he is found.' So the party began."

LUKE 15:24 NLT

Snuffy was gone for good.

Dan had jumped into his pickup truck and driven through town, over the river, and miles from home. He never thought to look in the truck bed where Snuffy lay curled up. When he returned home later that day, the family searched for their cat. But Snuffy was gone.

Six months later, Dan was again on the other end of town across the river. He spotted one of the scraggliest cats he'd ever seen.

"Snuffy!" his wife declared. Sure enough, the skinny, bedraggled, dirty bag of fur ran up to them when they stopped the truck. All three returned home in the safety of the truck cab.

Like the heartbroken father in Luke 15, God never stops pursuing those whom Jesus died to save—even when others have given up on them. As the psalmist tells us, we are never lost to God (see Psalm 139). He may find us bedraggled and wasted, but He embraces us.

Just as the father rejoiced and threw a party when his wandering son came home, Snuffy celebrated with loud meows until Dan pulled in the driveway. The lost was found!

Father, I pray for my family members who are far from You.
I pray that You would draw them to Yourself as only You can do.
Give them hearts to seek after You alone. Amen.

Ignoring God

"I love those who love me, and those who seek me find me."
PROVERBS 8:17 NIV

Emma ignores her human. She hides under beds, behind sofas, under cabinets... She's the ultimate introvert. That is, until she thinks her human is ignoring her. Then she's front and center, making sure her person knows she's there.

This means when Hannah tries to study for a test, Emma wants to take a nap on her study notes. When Hannah wants to watch television, Emma wants to meow in Hannah's ear. When Hannah wants to sleep, Emma will often crawl all over her.

In a lot of ways, we're all a little bit like Emma. We want to ignore God, going about our business without Him bothering us. We know He's there... and we want Him to leave us alone.

But the minute we actually feel God's absence, the moment we feel He's ignoring us, we realize that's not what we want at all. Then we're all up in His face, demanding attention, begging Him to remember that He loves us.

God never forgets us. He never stops loving us. But He does long for our companionship. He wants us to seek Him out because we love Him, not only because we want something from Him. Today and every day, we need to make time to express our affection for God, simply because He's our Master and we love Him.

Dear Father, forgive me for ignoring You.
I love You, and I want to show You every day.

Determination

Brethren, I count not myself to have apprehended: but this
one thing I do, forgetting those things which are behind,
and reaching forth unto those things which are before.

PHILIPPIANS 3:13 KJV

Tigger is aptly named. He believes himself to be a vicious great cat who can conquer the world. In reality, he's just a playful kitten whose world revolves around the pieces of straw that entertain him. For some reason, one piece of straw is never enough. Never mind that he tamed a piece a mere ten minutes ago. He is bent on bringing each piece into submission, and if you get in his way, you will experience the wrath of his tiny razor-like teeth. He is a determined little creature who, despite many accomplishments, is driven by other future goals.

There's something we can learn from Tigger's drive. So many times as Christians we do something for Christ, and we are satisfied. We dwell on our past accomplishments, or maybe we're focused on things in our path that scare us, so we don't bother to pursue future plans He has for us. This shouldn't be! There is so much to do before Jesus comes back. We can't let things get in the way of our serving Him. It's so imperative that we press onward. It's an exciting opportunity anyway—one we shouldn't squander. When this life is over, there will be a time of crowns and rewards and rest, but for now, keep in the battle!

Give me determination to continually
move forward in service to You!

Spending Quiet Time Together

"But when you pray, go into your room, close the door
and pray to your Father, who is unseen. Then your Father,
who sees what is done in secret, will reward you."

MATTHEW 6:6 NIV

Each morning, Allison sat down on the floor of her closet for quiet time with the Lord. She usually began by reading her Bible aloud. As soon as she began to speak, Jax, her brown tortoiseshell cat, came running to join her in the closet. She sat perfectly still, intently focused as Allison read, listening to each word.

Each morning it was the same. Jax sat, motionless, seldom moving a muscle the whole time. She was fixed on Allison's lips and the sound of her voice. It was as if she loved and respected the Word of God as much as Allison did.

Once she finished reading, she laid her open Bible down in front of her. Jax would move to position herself on top of the open Bible. She lay down on it as Allison prayed. A few times Allison would open her eyes and see Jax with her eyes closed, as if she were praying, too.

Lord, I love You and want to have a strong relationship
with You. I know time spent with You reading the
Bible and in prayer will help me know You more.
Give me a deep desire to study Your Word and pray.

Breathe

*Beloved, I pray that you may prosper in all
things and be in health, just as your soul prospers.*

3 JOHN 1:2 NKJV

The day felt demanding before first light ever cracked over the horizon. As I drove down the highway headed to a meeting on this very cold day, the sunrise warmed me. My driving prayers of request became prayers of gratitude. That didn't stop the day from stacking up with difficult conversation and unexpected challenges at work. In the midst of it all, one of my friends texted—she was going through a rough time, and I barely had a moment to offer a couple words in response. My husband called and needed some scheduling information as soon as I could get back to him. My son texted our great need for groceries. *Breathe. . .* I told myself. By the time I got to the end of the day and made it home with a few bags from the market, I wanted to collapse.

Sitting down to take my shoes off shifted my focus—there lay my cat curled up on the rug with some other shoes. He looked up, smiled lazily with his eyes, and began to purr softly. I was clearly jealous of him. I didn't like getting dealt the crazy day I'd had. But in this simple moment, my cat reminded me to slow down and just be present.

God, thank You for simple moments
and for growing me through it all.

Country Life, Country Kitties

It is a good thing to give thanks unto the LORD,
and to sing praises unto thy name, O Most High.
PSALM 92:1 KJV

Carl and Alice live in a refurbished farmhouse in rural Pennsylvania. The kids, when they visit, lovingly call it "the old barn." The place is warm and cozy, Carl's son admits, but he'd like to see the retired couple move closer to the city. Maybe to a condo within a ten-minute drive of a hospital—just in case.

His dad scoffs at that. "We have 911 service here. If we give up the house, Alice has to give up her ten cats."

"Oh, so they're *my* cats, are they?" Alice jokes to her husband. "You're the one who'd be crying over leaving Sunny behind." The couple gazes lovingly at a fat orange cat sprawled on the rug. The animal opens one eyelid as if it knows it's being talked about.

The couple's son says, "I can start placing them now. Two here, two there. They'll be happy, I promise."

"Not Trinket." Alice cuddles a dark-striped tabby who nestles against her arm and vibrates. "This kitty needs country air."

Their son laughs. "You mean *you* need country air, Mom." He hugs his parents. "Okay, you and the kitties have everything under control. This is a good place for you to be right now. 'Nuff said."

Lord, we give You thanks for all the little blessings of life—
concerned family, animal companionship,
and the care we show for each other.

Fraidy Cat

In God I trust and am not afraid.
What can man do to me?
PSALM 56:11 NIV

Black Purrl is a fraidy cat. She is seven pounds of spider-catching, long-jumping, dog-bossing spunk, and she knows it. BP, as we call her, will sit on the windowsill and frighten the neighbor's mastiff out of his wits with her unblinking stare.

Like all brave souls, BP does have an Achilles' heel—the vacuum. As soon as I roll it out of the closet, she scoots backward, crouched low to the floor, tail twitching nervously. When I hit the power button, she makes a frantic dash for the studio, leaps onto the desk, and cowers behind the computer monitor until the horrible beast is once again banished to its lair. To BP, the vacuum is not a tool; it's an unfathomable mystery. It is large, loud, and unpredictable.

Her reaction to the vacuum reminds me of Judges 7, which tells the story of Gideon and his army of 300 men. The Midianites numbered over 100,000 soldiers and did not know such a tiny force opposed them. They never even saw Gideon's army. They feared the noise created by sounding trumpets and breaking pitchers. Overwhelmed by harmless racket, they fled in terror, and God gave His people victory.

Dear Lord, give me discernment to filter out
the sounds of those who wish to cause me fear.
Help me hear Your quiet voice in the din of daily life.

Eye Level

Humble yourselves, therefore, under God's mighty hand,
that he may lift you up in due time.

1 PETER 5:6 NIV

Vanna liked to be at eye level with her humans. Actually, when possible, she chose to look down on them, as if to make sure everyone in the room understood who was really in charge. The only time she walked on the ground was when there was no furniture or shelf to take her where she needed to go.

Often, we want to be at eye level with God. We may acknowledge Him as Lord with our mouths, but our hearts want to maintain complete control. We don't want to place ourselves below the God of the universe, because that requires humility. And humility is hard, even when it comes to God.

But when we place ourselves at God's level, we're really telling God we don't trust Him. We don't need Him. We feel we can do a better job at running things than He can.

The problem is, we can't do a better job than God because we're not God. We're not at His level. The sooner we learn to humble ourselves before Him and let Him have complete control of our lives, the sooner we will feel His love, compassion, and blessings poured out on our lives.

Dear Father, forgive me for placing myself at Your level.
I know I'm not capable of doing Your job. I love You.
I trust You, and I know You are good.

A Panther's Bite

Be sober, be vigilant; because your adversary the devil,
as a roaring lion, walketh about, seeking whom he may devour.
1 PETER 5:8 KJV

Most of the cats I had when I was growing up were actually strays.
They came and went as they pleased, and if I could manage to catch
and tame them, I was happy enough with that. One of these cats
was black, so I called him Panther. He lived up to his name quite
well. One day I went to feed him, and he thought he'd have my hand
for dinner. He wasn't mean, just hungry, but I had no idea where
he'd come from. I didn't know if he'd been vaccinated or if he had
rabies. So I worried. Then I'd remind myself that he looked quite
healthy and that his temperament was certainly not that of a rabid
animal. Then I'd worry, and the cycle continued until I realized that
both of us were just fine.

Panther's bite was vicious and left its mark, but it was nothing
like the damage Satan's attacks can do to us. I wasn't prepared that
day to be bitten, and so often we're not prepared to be devoured by
Satan. He approaches from all sides, looking for our weakest area.
His great desire is to see us fall out of fellowship with Christ and to
become ineffective in our witness.

We need to determine to be on guard, to be ready to resist him
when the battle comes (James 4:7).

Lord, guard me. Protect me from the roar of Satan.

Time to Connect

When he came and had seen the grace of God, he was glad,
and encouraged them all that with purpose of heart
they should continue with the Lord.

ACTS 11:23 NKJV

Over the past few days, Kay thought about calling her cousin, Penny. Each time she excused the idea for one reason or another—the length of her to-do list, the three-hour difference in time between them, and the unwanted conversation of how she was doing after her husband's death.

Kay walked through the living room, picking up the toys her gray tabby, Bubba, had left all over the room. She caught a glimpse of the edge of her phone underneath him as he rolled over in her chair. "Bubba, what are you doing on my phone?" she asked rhetorically as she reached to pick it up from underneath him. Surprised, her phone was active. It was calling someone—her cousin, Penny. She could hear Penny on the other end. "Kay? Kay? Hello?"

"Oh my goodness," Kay said, bringing her phone up to her ear. "I can't believe it, but Bubba called you. He was lying on my phone."

Penny's laughter brought a smile to Kay's face, something she hadn't done in a while. "Guess Bubba knew we needed to chat," Penny replied. "It's so good to hear your voice."

Heavenly Father, forgive me when I procrastinate in doing something I know I need to do. Give me strength to face the hard things and be obedient to You.

Divine Nickname

"I have summoned you by name; you are mine."
ISAIAH 43:1 NIV

Cats come in all kinds of colors, sizes, and personalities. And I'm sure each of us cat owners figures we have the most beautiful, brilliant, or unusual cat of all. Our calico cat, Snickers, was very dear to us, despite all her quirks, messiness, and behavioral problems.

We often called her Psycho-Cat because sometimes she seemed to be a little off. At times, she'd race up and down the hallway as if her tail was on fire, even climbing the walls clear to the ceiling. She was a little psychotic in other ways, too. She treated my son like he was her kitten. She'd yip at him until he followed her. He's six foot two and close to 250 pounds. We called him Big Kitty.

Revelation 2:17 says those who overcome in the last days will receive a name that only God knows, written on a white stone. How wonderful it would be to have a name that God Himself gives. I'm sure it won't be as goofy as Psycho-Cat or Big Kitty. Or maybe it will be. God knows our quirks, messiness, and behavior problems, and He still loves us.

Father, thank You that You know all about me,
even my secret thoughts, and You still love me.

Swallow This or Else!

Wounds from a sincere friend are
better than many kisses from an enemy.
PROVERBS 27:6 NLT

This test of wills came about annually. In his hand Mark held the deworming pill. Opposite him sat Coyote, daring him to make him swallow the dreaded cure. Over the years, Mark had tried everything. He thought about buying some body armor for this year's battle, but the cost changed his mind.

"I read you should wrap the cat up snugly in a bath towel," his wife suggested.

Mark wrapped Coyote tightly in a towel and held him firmly against his chest while prying open his mouth. His wife put the pill in Coyote's mouth; Mark clamped it shut. Coyote did not purr passively or cooperate. Surprisingly, in spite of pill-saturated cat spit everywhere and Mark sporting some bloody scratches, the cure worked for another year.

Sometimes what's bitter serves only to make us better. Whether we're passed over for a promotion at work, or our strong-willed child disobeys us yet again, or insurance didn't cover the bill as we had expected, troubles come. Our challenge is not to become bitter and lash out at others.

Can you do that in whatever you're facing today? *Will* you do it?

Dear Lord, I'm in a place I don't want to be.
I'm disappointed and frustrated. Please help me
grasp the peace You offer even though I don't
know how to do that right now. Help me, my God. Amen.

Making a Difference

He said to them, "Go into all the world
and preach the gospel to all creation."
MARK 16:15 NIV

Ellie is a brave cat. . .especially when there's a pane of glass between her and her prey. She likes to pounce on small bugs and birds that land on the other side of the window. She spends most of the day on the ledge, tail dangling contentedly, keeping watch over all the comings and goings, keeping her home safe from tiny predators.

But if one of them makes it past the doorway, she ignores them. Her guard-cat skills are just pretend, to make her feel important. When given the opportunity to really work, to really make a difference, she yawns and loses interest.

That's what happens with many Christians today. We like to perch on a pew on Sunday morning. We wear our Christian T-shirts; we place Christian bumper stickers on our cars. But when we're faced with the opportunity to truly go to battle, to make a difference, we yawn and turn away. We're kind of like Ellie; we want to feel important, but we don't want to actually do anything.

Those are normal human feelings. Nobody wants to work harder than we must, or place ourselves in uncomfortable situations. But God's call on our lives is not one of passive self-importance. It's a call to action: to love, to get involved, to make a difference.

Dear Father, help me to make a positive difference in
the lives of those around me, even if it's inconvenient.

Is There Anything You Need?

A time to weep and a time to laugh,
a time to mourn and a time to dance.
ECCLESIASTES 3:4 NIV

Nicole got the news at work that a close family member had died. She asked for a week off to attend the funeral, which was local. Her supervisor granted the request and soon word spread around Nicole's workplace about this loss in her life. Coworkers stopped by her work station to express their sympathy and ask, "Is there anything you need?"

"Thanks, I'll be okay," she told them. "I'm just trying to get through the rest of the day. I can't really think straight right now. You can imagine."

Three different people asked, "How about your cats? Do you need somebody to watch them while you're busy with the funeral?"

Nicole was touched by this, by the fact that her coworkers were extending their concern for her to her dear pets. "They'll be fine," she explained. "I'll be out a lot with family. But I'll be home every morning and evening to feed the cats. That's really nice of you to offer."

"You be sure and let us know if you need help," these kind people assured her.

Nicole received several sympathy gifts for her pets. Those sending them worried that the cats would be alone too much, and so they mailed "a little something" to tide them over during a tough time.

Lord, touch our hearts and show us where
a little kindness can go a long way.

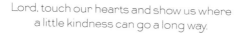

Feed Those Cats

So when they had dined, Jesus saith to Simon Peter, Simon, son of
Jonas, lovest thou me more than these? He saith unto him, Yea, Lord;
thou knowest that I love thee. He saith unto him, Feed my lambs.

JOHN 21:15 KJV

It seems there are always a bunch of cats on my porch. I might have invited one of them. Evidently he invited others, because before too long, several more had moved in. They're a noisy bunch when they get hungry, so we try to keep that from happening. Several of our children especially love feeding the cats, so it's not too hard to give them that job. I'm glad they are so willing.

Jesus had a job for Peter to do, but first He needed Peter to examine himself. He needed Peter to decide if he truly loved his Master or if there was something that came between them. Three times Jesus questioned Peter. "Peter, do you love Me more than these?" Three times Peter answered, "Lord, You know I love You." Three times Jesus said, "If you love Me, I have a work for you to do."

If I truly love Jesus, He has work for me to do, too. It's a daily examination, though. If there's something between Jesus and me, I need to turn it over to Him first. Only then can He use me effectively.

Lord. I love You. What would You have me do?

Sitting with the Humans

"Come to Me, all you who labor and are heavy laden, and I will give you rest. Take My yoke upon you and learn from Me, for I am gentle and lowly in heart, and you will find rest for your souls. For My yoke is easy and My burden is light."
MATTHEW 11:28–30 NKJV

Our big cat, Bruce, does this thing where he sits on the floor against the wall, looking rather humanish. It can really startle you if you round the corner and find him there, flaring a leg out for a stretch. I've jumped a little sideways before.

One particularly long day after dinner, three of us sat talking at the table for a while. There were weighty decisions to discuss and difficult days ahead. Bruce hopped up on an empty chair, leaned back and positioned himself upright against the chair back. Eyes wide with disbelief, we all started laughing. Who does that? I mean, what *cat* does that?! Bruce, that's who. It was just the comic relief we needed during a heavy time.

Lord, thank You for lifting the heavy burdens for me, even if it means simply giving me laughter to carry me through from time to time. Take today's load, too. I am grateful that You want to.

Demon or Angel?

*I am convinced that nothing can ever separate us from
God's love. Neither death nor life, neither angels nor demons,
neither our fears for today nor our worries about tomorrow—
not even the powers of hell can separate us from God's love.*

ROMANS 8:38 NLT

Our daughter was house- and cat-sitting while our son worked out
of the country for an extended period of time. The house was fine.
But Riggs, the cat, didn't appreciate Deb's presence. He was only a
few months old, yet from the first time they met, Riggs acted hostile.
She loved cats; he didn't reciprocate.

Every time Deb entered the house, Riggs greeted her with
snarly hisses, arched his back, and went into attack mode. She tried
everything to show him she wanted to be his friend, but nothing
worked. Her only comfort was that he didn't like anybody very much.

Riggs refused to play with her, though he was willing to eat
treats from her hand. He grew beyond the cute kitten stage, and we
thought surely he would also outgrow his frosty attitude, but their
relationship didn't improve. He might as well have worn demon
horns and carried a pitchfork.

A year later, as soon as our son returned, Riggs became the
perfect pet. He seemed to sprout angel wings and a halo overnight!

Heavenly Father, You continually reach out to show Your love.
Help me never to be unresponsive or unappreciative.
I want to always please You with my attitude.

What You Say Matters

Death and life are in the power of the tongue:
and they that love it shall eat the fruit thereof.
PROVERBS 18:21 KJV

Since their move to a new city, Annie noticed her son Josh's sudden outbursts of anger occurring more often. She learned with her first son that those eleventh and twelfth years of life proved difficult as bodies grew too fast, causing their owners to come across as awkward. She caught Josh using off-color language a couple of times and spoke with him about it. Still, he struggled to get a handle on his emotions.

One afternoon, she heard words she didn't like coming from the living room. She rounded the corner and stopped. She saw Josh in the chair with their cat, Izzy, in his lap. Izzy seemed to be "correcting" him. Anna would have guessed that Izzy would have run from Josh when he became angry. Instead, she climbed up into his lap and placed her paws over his lips as if to gently say, "Close your mouth. No talking. Shhh!"

Over the next few months, instead of correcting Josh, she went to the Lord in prayer and continued to watch as Izzy silently helped Josh get a handle on his words and his emotions.

Lord, sometimes words boil over. I don't like for my emotions to have control of me. Help me to remember that what I say really matters. I will choose my words wisely.

Chasing the Light

Take delight in the LORD, and he will
give you the desires of your heart.

PSALM 37:4 NIV

Cats are fascinating creatures, as evidenced by the multitude of cat videos on social media. Our calico cat, Snickers, may have been an Internet sensation if I would have filmed her. She would go crazy over reflected light.

We would take a CD or something shiny and bounce the reflected light off the walls and furniture. We would watch in amusement as she danced around on her hind legs like a meerkat, chirping like a canary as she pursued it. Of course, when she did manage to tap the spot with her paw, there was nothing there. She would look a little confused—all that excitement and energy expended for nothing.

It's like us humans with temptation. We chase after those things that look attractive, speaking and behaving in ways contrary to a godly nature. When we catch them, we find nothing of value, or worse than nothing. When we sin, we're trying to please ourselves in our own way, rather than allowing God to bless us in His way as we obey Him. Instead of bright, shiny things, let us chase after Jesus, the True Light.

Dear Lord, help me focus on You and not
be distracted by the world's enticements,
trusting You to grant the desires of my heart.

A Midnight Escape

How shall we escape, if we neglect so great salvation;
which at the first began to be spoken by the Lord,
and was confirmed unto us by them that heard him...?

HEBREWS 2:3 KJV

Midnight came to me as a grown cat, and we sort of adopted one another. I felt that if she was going to take up permanent residence, she should be checked by the veterinarian, so my dad scheduled an appointment. It just so happened that I had a scheduled activity at the time of her appointment, so my younger brother went with my dad to hold Midnight in the car.

When they stepped out of the car, something frightened Midnight, and she leaped from my brother's grasp and darted across a busy road. He was unable to go after her because of an oncoming truck.

Perhaps a noise scared her, or it could be she knew that needles awaited her. At any rate, Midnight escaped the torture of the vet's office.

The wrath of God far exceeds the pain of vaccinations. On our own, we can't escape sin and hell, but God has provided a great salvation. Through the blood of His only Son, Jesus, we can have salvation. God is just and holy; He cannot look upon the sin that condemns us, but He is also loving and merciful. If we accept salvation through the death, burial, and resurrection of His Son, He will cleanse us from our sins.

O God, draw one who desires an
escape from sin to Yourself today.

Love Curled Up beside Me

"The LORD your God in your midst, The Mighty One, will save;
He will rejoice over you with gladness, He will quiet you
with His love, He will rejoice over you with singing."
ZEPHANIAH 3:17 NKJV

Ever have one of those days when you just need to crawl into bed to feel warm and comforted? Well, it was one of those days for me.

Thankfully, right after work I was able to lie down and rest for a while, which doesn't always happen. I dropped the bags of groceries in the kitchen, my jacket on a chair, and fell out of my shoes into bed just as tears started to roll down my cheeks. Some days my human relationships just aren't where I'd like them to be and it's painful, but thank God He knows. My jet black cat, Jak, followed me all the way in, curled up beside me, quiet and calm. It's times like these that it feels a lot like God's love curling up next to me. God's good that way, not only ministering through His Spirit, but through the animals He's placed in my care as well.

Lord, thank You for Your great love that knows no bounds.
Even through Your creation You offer Your love to me.

The Mortician's Cat

Do not be misled: "Bad company corrupts good character."
1 CORINTHIANS 15:33 NIV

"Just what do you think you're doing?"

Don had had a busy day at the mortuary. Living and dead bodies coming in and going out had left the mortician feeling little better than near dead himself. He still had mounds of paperwork to get through, so he had come home to finish it up. Enter Jingles, his wife's three-legged cat.

In spite of the car accident that had left him maimed, Jingles had adjusted well and now walks around effortlessly. He jumps effortlessly, too—which is just what he did as he jumped up on Don's lap to make himself comfortable.

Don continued to protest. "Michelle, your cat's in here!"

Over Don's protests, Jingles settled in for a nap. Hearing no response from his wife, Don shrugged and picked up his pen again. He absentmindedly stroked Jingles. *Hmmmm. Soft.*

Jingles takes his naps on Don's lap regularly now. The mortician no longer dismisses his purring companion.

"Jingles is one cool cat."

A human lap is a perfect settling-in spot for a cat, but we need to be careful in our choice of where and with whom we spend time. We don't want to ostracize people different from us, but we want to be wise in our choice of companions. After all, those whom we spend the most time with will have the greatest impact on our character.

Father, I thank You for the friends I have. I pray to be a good friend in return who encourages and blesses others. In Jesus' name, amen.

Chosen by God

Blessed is the nation whose God is the LORD,
the people He has chosen as His own inheritance.
PSALM 33:12 NKJV

Adoption day had finally arrived, and I knew exactly the type of cat I wanted: a big black tomcat with great green eyes and a cuddly disposition. I practically ran through the store to get to the adoption area. By the time my husband caught up to me, I was staring into the cages, and the cats were staring back. Siamese, marmalade, and calico kittens tumbled and purred while a few mama cats lazed on carpet squares. There were no black cats—and no toms at all. Just then, my husband tapped my shoulder and I turned around to see a tiny brown nose and big fuzzy ears peeping out of his large, gentle hand. "I love this one," he said.

My first thought was *It's not even a whole cat!* I held the tiny tabby kitten and fell in love. I no longer wanted a big black tomcat. The adoption worker said the kitten had been rescued from a rain gutter and wasn't very trustful of people yet. Two hours later, the kitten had been renamed "Black Purrl" and was settled into my study, busily destroying my leather briefcase. In less than a day, she was family. She had learned to trust those who had chosen her.

Thank You, God, for choosing me. Help me to
rely on Your provision for my every need. Amen.

The Cat in the Mirror

*Therefore, if anyone is in Christ, the new creation has come:
The old has gone, the new is here!*

2 CORINTHIANS 5:17 NIV

Pixie had a favorite playmate—herself. She loved to climb on the bathroom counter and admire the cat in the mirror. For hours, she'd meow and sing and converse with the elusive cat who watched her just as closely, mewed in unison, and would never jump over the wall to cuddle with her.

Pixie was happy with whom she saw in the mirror.

When I look at myself, I'd love to be that content with the person looking back at me. I'm learning that I need to be gentle with myself and see myself the way God sees me—as a beloved child.

On my own, I'll never be the wise, kind, compassionate, generous creature I'd like to be. But with God, all things are possible. The more time I spend in His Word and in prayer, the more I start to reflect His image. And the more I look like Him, the more beautiful I appear to everyone around me—even the person in the mirror.

Dear Father, please help me to see myself the way You see me,
as a cherished child. Help me to become more like You
every day, so the image people see when they look at
my heart reflects Your beauty and love.

Can I Show You a Kindness?

Rejoice with those who rejoice;
mourn with those who mourn.
ROMANS 12:15 NIV

A church friend of mine, Miriam, was feeling overwhelmed over the passing of two of her cats. They were senior cats and had lived good, long lives. Knowing that didn't lessen her grief. Losing one right after the other left a big hole in her life.

She hid her sadness because she felt people who weren't cat owners wouldn't understand. Someone actually told her, "It's just a cat. Go get another one." She gently told the person it wasn't that easy to get past the death of a beloved pet. Another friend kindly said, "I'll pray for you. I'll pray you remember only the good times."

Miriam thanked her, then e-mailed me in tears. "I remember *all* the times I had with Misty and Frederick, even when I wanted to boot them out the door. I start crying for no reason. Is there something wrong with me?"

I knew where she was coming from and was able to sympathize. We sent e-mails back and forth where we talked about the funny little things our pets had done over the years. "Hugs to you," I wrote at the end of my short e-mails of encouragement. Miriam needed to talk, and I was there to listen online. That helped her to heal.

Lord, aid us in choosing the right words for the right person at the right time. Let us always show your gentle spirit to others in need.

Lovely among the Gray

Wherefore come out from among them, and be ye separate, saith the Lord, and touch not the unclean thing; and I will receive you.

2 CORINTHIANS 6:17 KJV

One would think that with as many cats as we have on our farm there would be some variety of color, but among the ones that have chosen to live at our house, that just isn't the case. We see a lot of gray. The kids claim to be able to tell them apart, but I just see gray.

Then there's Lovely. She stands out because she's brown. I can easily pick her out in the crowd. She's noticeable for other reasons as well. She's independent and self-sufficient. She's a good mother and overall a very nice cat.

It's not that the other cats aren't decent. They're pretty cats and nice enough, but they all sort of blend together. Sadly, that's like many Christians. They're nice enough individuals, but they blend in with the world so much that no one knows the difference. This should not be. God calls us to separate ourselves from the world. If we want to make a difference, we have to be different. It's so easy to say, "I'm not doing anything wrong, so I must be okay." It might be true, but do those around you even know you are saved? If not, won't you come out from among them?

Dear God, please show me how to make a difference.

Bold and Courageous

I've commanded you to be strong and brave.
Don't ever be afraid or discouraged! I am the LORD
your God, and I will be there to help you wherever you go.

JOSHUA 1:9 CEV

"Did you get your mom all moved into the new place?" Carrie asked her friend, Charla.

"Yes! Mom and her fearless cat, Gretel," Charla smiled. "I thought she'd hide for a week, but instead, she came right out of her cat taxi and started exploring the house."

"Well, that's great."

"Yes, Mom is happy about it now, but last night she called me frantic because she couldn't find Gretel. She walked all through the house while I stayed with her on the phone. Suddenly, she looked up and saw that Gretel was in the far corner of the roofline, asleep. She had walked across one of the beams that crosses from the second story to the kitchen. It's a two-by-two-foot beam. Gretel's suddenly very adventurous."

"Some cats have no fear—especially of heights," Carrie replied. "I wish I could be bold and courageous like that when I have to step out of my comfort zone."

Charla encouraged her friend. "God has called us to be strong and courageous. We don't have to fear any situation. He's promised to be with us to help us."

Father, You are always with me. You created me to be
bold and courageous. I don't have to be afraid, but instead
I can step out in faith knowing You are with me.

Drawing Near

Come near to God and he will come near to you.
JAMES 4:8 NIV

Cats tend to come on their own terms. It's not up to the owner to govern a cat's behavior. They do what they want to, whenever they're good and ready. Our calico cat, Snickers, would come running at the sound of the can opener.

At times, Snickers was snooty. She didn't want anyone to pick her up, but when I sat on my recliner tapping away on my laptop, she demanded attention. We'd have our morning battles of her competing with the computer screen. At times, I wrote looking between her ears with my hands coming out from underneath her like crabs scrambling to the ocean.

Sometimes when we approach God, we behave like cats, only coming to Him when we're good and ready to, usually when we're in trouble or have some physical or emotional problem. Jesus died on the cross so we can "approach God's throne of grace with confidence, so that we may receive mercy and find grace to help us in our time of need" (Hebrews 4:16). However, we don't have to wait until we're in trouble to approach God. We can draw near in worship and thanksgiving, like a cat curls up on his person's lap.

Father, I draw near to You in worship, thanksgiving, and affection. Forgive me for those times Your Spirit draws me near and I opt for a TV show.

Given to Gluttony

Put a knife to your throat if you are given to gluttony.
PROVERBS 23:2 NIV

Big felines like lions and Siberian tigers can tip the scales at over five hundred pounds and just under a half a ton, respectively. Lion tamers and others who work with these cats do well to remember that weight alone puts the human at a disadvantage.

Betty's domestic cats carry a lot of bulk themselves. Frieda weighs fourteen pounds. Sandy betters Frieda by one pound, but Oliver beats them both at his formidable twenty pounds. I'm not sure if these cats overeat, are overfed, or just happen to be very weighty domestic felines by breeding, but few dogs tangle with them.

Many people struggle with gluttony. Not just gluttony when it comes to food, but overindulgence in any of a host of appetites. Addiction to prescription drugs, television, sports, or even buying shoes shows an appetite out of control. Excess is unhealthy and unwise. We're told: "Let your moderation be known unto all men." Why? Not for wisdom or health reasons, but because "The Lord is at hand" (Philippians 4:5 KJV).

The first thing I need to do if I have an appetite gone wild is to confess it as sin. Only then can God get control of what is controlling me.

Father God, You know better than me what I'm struggling with. I ask for Your forgiveness. I pray to seek You for the satisfaction I crave. In Jesus' powerful name I pray, amen.

Defining Fear

"The fear of the LORD is the beginning of wisdom,
and the knowledge of the Holy One is understanding.
For by me your days will be multiplied."

PROVERBS 9:10–11 NKJV

Eva gives our family fresh definitions of fear on a regular basis. Recently, she was walking out into the backyard until she encountered a little breeze that made her cower. Carefully making her way back to the house from only four feet away, she darted through the door that I, grinning, was still holding open.

Another time I let her out the front door where she promptly saw a flock of birds coming overhead. She tore to the front door and held her face very close to the storm glass, squeaking with an expression that screamed, *Let me in!*

It makes me realize how different each of our perspectives is, with our own perceptions, wounds, weaknesses, and willingness to respond to help that is offered. One thing we know is that no matter where we find ourselves, we can put our trust in God.

Lord, give me the understanding that I need for my life today,
and thank You for knowing exactly what I need.

Are You Listening?

So faith comes from hearing, that is,
hearing the Good News about Christ.
ROMANS 10:17 NLT

Danielle took a deep breath and listened. Silence. She enjoyed those moments right after her husband left to take the kids to school. She walked into the living room and opened the blinds to the morning sun. Muffin, her beautiful cream puff of a cat, lay curled up on the couch. As the blinds rolled up, she twitched her ears to the sound.

Danielle looked at her. Although Muffin's eyes were shut, Danielle knew she was listening. She was constantly alert, aware of anything going on—anywhere in the house. Anytime their furnace clicked on or the dishwasher came on, her ears perked up. Sometimes Danielle would catch her staring off into the distance. Although Danielle couldn't hear anything, she noticed Muffin's ears twitched and swiveled.

Picking up her Bible, Danielle switched on the overhead lamp, careful not to disturb Muffin. In the quiet, she turned the pages of her Bible and whispered quietly to God. "I'm here," she said. "I'm listening. What do you have for me today?"

Lord, life is busy and loud. Remind me to take quiet moments throughout the day and listen. Help me to be more aware of what is going on in the world around me and what You are speaking to me. I don't want to miss a single thing.

The Unlovable

And when they saw it, they all murmured, saying,
That he was gone to be guest with a man that is a sinner.
LUKE 19:7 KJV

Histy was not with us long, as he was involved in an accident that cut his life short. He did leave a lasting impression, however. He was a pretty kitten, and my daughter fell in love with him immediately. He did not return her affection, however. He was a mean little thing. If anyone would get near him, he'd begin to hiss immediately, and if you continued to get closer, he'd begin to swat with his paw as if he were some invincible lion. Most of us weren't terribly interested in befriending him. My daughter continued to try, and cautiously he would let her get closer. While he never did become a playful, cuddly kitten, he did finally accept her.

There are many people in the world who are mean or grouchy or hurting. Maybe they are the perfect example of "desperately wicked" people (Jeremiah 17:9). They are the people Jesus came to save. So many times we turn our backs on them. This should not be! Christ is our example. He's who we strive to be like, and He reaches out to these people, saying, "Come. Let Me change your life!" We must show them His love. We must reach out to them and give them the Gospel. We must love the unlovable.

Jesus, help me not to be so proud that
I lose sight of my purpose here.

We're All Family

*Gracious words are a honeycomb,
sweet to the soul and healing to the bones.*

PROVERBS 16:24 NIV

Laura tried to be friendly to everyone in her office, but there was one woman who didn't warm to her at all. Maybe it was the difference in their ages. Laura was just out of school. Kathryn had twenty years at the firm. The long-term employee was professional but reserved whenever Laura tried to engage her in conversation.

One day, Laura had to deliver some papers to Kathryn at her cubicle where she noticed a digital photo frame. The featured photo showed a cat with long hair, a brown face, and white fur around the ears, collar, and chest. "That's adorable," Laura commented. "What kind of cat is it?"

Kathryn looked up with a smile. "It's a Himalayan. That's my son's cat."

"Does he live with you?" Laura asked. That opened up the conversation for Kathryn to relate that no, her son and his wife lived in Boston, but they were driving down to leave the cat with Mom while they took a vacation.

"They won't trust their cat with anyone but me," Kathryn said with pride. "After all, we're all family."

This started a dialogue that Laura made sure to build on as the weeks went on. She was thankful that she'd finally found a topic to get their conversation flowing.

O Lord, let our words reflect the principles of our faith as we strive to be on good terms with everyone.

Rewarded

And without faith it is impossible to please God,
because anyone who comes to him must believe that he
exists and that he rewards those who earnestly seek him.
HEBREWS 11:6 NIV

Our cat, Hudson, is the consummate hunter. Mice, birds, moles—even flies and butterflies—seldom escape once he spots them. His persistence over long minutes often gives him his reward.

Hudson anticipates reward for his hunting prowess. Many mornings we pat him on the head and commend him for a dead carcass on our front porch. It stays there until he hears "Atta boy," too. He works hard for his reward and expects it.

We may feel uncomfortable talking about heavenly rewards, but God doesn't shy away from the topic. Numerous times in the Bible we're told to work for that which the Lord delights to reward.

"Serve wholeheartedly. . .you know that the Lord will reward each one for whatever good they do" (Ephesians 6:7, 8). "He [Moses] was looking ahead to his reward" (Hebrews 11:26). "Watch out that you do not lose what we have worked for, but that you may be rewarded fully" (2 John 8).

If we reward a good mouser for a job well done, how much more will our gracious God reward those "who earnestly seek him."

Thank You, Lord God, that You know all of
my heart and life and promise me the reward
of Yourself and more to come. Amen.

Keeping Watch

The LORD will keep you from all harm—
he will watch over your life.
PSALM 121:7 NIV

Tom Kitty may have been a tom, but he wasn't very tough. He was a lover, not a fighter. Unfortunately, there was a big ol' mean, tough cat that lived in the woods nearby. About once a month, that bully cat would show up looking for a fight, and Tom Kitty usually came away with lots of scratches and cuts.

One day, Rick heard a noise in the backyard. He moved the curtain aside, and the feral cat looked up. Rick locked eyes with the cat, and in an instant, the bully was over the fence and back into the woods where he belonged. Tom Kitty never knew what happened.

Sometimes our enemy leaves some nasty scratches and cuts on our lives. But how many times does our heavenly Father lock eyes with Satan and send him running back where he belongs? God will protect us if we stay close to Him. Oh, we may get a few bangs and bruises, but if we belong to God, if we trust Christ as our Savior, the injuries are only temporary. No matter how bad the fight may seem, we know we're on the winning team.

Dear Father, thank You for protecting me. Remind me to stay close to You and to trust in Your watchful care.

Relentless

*"I say to you, though he will not rise and give to him
because he is his friend, yet because of his persistence
he will rise and give him as many as he needs."*
LUKE 11:8 NKJV

Our Mr. Katniss is the definition of persistent love. As I write this on the front porch, he is relentlessly crawling all over me and nuzzling me while he happily purrs. I put him down nicely so I could make progress on my story, and he jumped right back up. I gave him some attention and then was firmer with the putting-him-down part. He was firmer with the getting back up. He can't understand why I don't just use my hands to massage him rather than keep them on my keyboard. I ended up going in the house.

I could be frustrated, which is easy to do, or I can remember how much Katniss gives me a fraction of the picture of God's persistence and love toward me. God is absolutely relentless in pursuing my heart. He loves me that much.

Lord, help me not only to see Your love for me,
but to accept it and reflect it for others who need it, too.

A Place to Belong

Furthermore, because we are united with Christ, we have received an inheritance from God, for he chose us in advance, and he makes everything work out according to his plan.
EPHESIANS 1:11 NLT

Shortly after we moved to Indiana from sunny Arizona, we noticed a male kitten, probably just shy of a year old, hanging around our backyard. We assumed someone had dumped him off in our neighborhood. We already had a cat and a dog, and our neighbors had three cats, but we weren't going to let him starve.

He had a sweet attitude and wanted attention from people. Over the next few weeks, my mom called him "Visitor Kitty." He had no home, really. As he gained weight and strength, he also proved to be a great hunter. He entertained us in the afternoons by creeping into the wooded area by our home and emerging minutes later with his prey.

As the leaves began to fall, we knew "Visitor Kitty" needed a place to belong. One afternoon our neighbor came over to say he'd found someone willing to give the kitten a home. His hunting skill would prove beneficial on this family's farm. He would have plenty to eat and a permanent place where he belonged.

Like "Visitor Kitty," it's so good to have a place to call home. God gives that to us when we trust in Christ—a place in His family and an eternal home with Him.

Heavenly Father, You have given me a place
in Your family. I know I belong to You. I am
Yours and You are mine for all eternity.

That's My Blanket

*Command those who are rich in this present age not
to be haughty, nor to trust in uncertain riches but in
the living God, who gives us richly all things to enjoy.*

1 TIMOTHY 6:17 NKJV

Cats abound at animal shelters. They plead, with lonesome eyes
and sometimes a mournful cry, for someone to take them home and
become their forever family. There are at least half a dozen everyone
falls in love with, so whittling the choices down to one isn't easy.

Our adult daughter called me from the shelter, "There's a gray
tiger I really like. What do you think?"

"Um. . . I'm at work and have no idea. He'll be your
responsibility, so choose carefully."

Kris selected Hobbes and brought him directly to the office
for my approval. After riding several miles in a strange car, Hobbes
walked in and immediately curled up under my desk, content as
could be. When she took him home, he acted like he'd owned it all
his life.

Hobbes was not a cuddly kitty. He would rather crouch behind
a couch than snuggle. So I felt really special when I visited one day
and he jumped onto my lap as soon as I sat down.

Kris laughed, "Don't get too excited, Mom. You're sitting on his
blanket, and he wants it back."

Dear Lord, help me never to hang on to things so
much that I can't share them with others. Help me
always remember that everything I have is a gift
from You and You delight in Your children who
are cheerful givers (2 Corinthians 9:7).

The Only First Cat

Nevertheless I have somewhat against thee,
because thou hast left thy first love.

REVELATION 2:4 KJV

A person can only ever have one "very first cat." Truly, I don't remember how old I was when I got my first cat. I do know it was at Thanksgiving. We were at my Grandpa's house, and he had chosen a dark gray kitten with four white paws just for me. It was my dream come true! I couldn't decide if I should name him Mittens for his four white paws or Smoky for his sooty color, so he became Mittens Smoke. That night I proudly rode all the way home with him in the very back of our station wagon. It was one of the happiest days of my life. I've had quite a few cats since that time, but none will ever be able to share that first spot with Mittens. He will always be the best very first cat.

How special to have a first cat, but what about our first love? Only Jesus rightfully deserves that place in our lives. At some point most of us are guilty of allowing something else to become more important than Christ, but He should have the preeminence. Our families, our jobs, hobbies, yes, even our churches, are good things, but when they come between us and our Lord, we have left our first love. It is time to return!

Search me, O God! Show me the idols that need to be removed from my heart so that I can return to my first love.

Always Right Side Up

*No temptation has overtaken you except what is common to
mankind. And God is faithful; he will not let you be tempted
beyond what you can bear. But when you are tempted,
he will also provide a way out so that you can endure it.*

1 CORINTHIANS 10:13 NIV

I heard others say cats always land on their feet, but Sassy, our gray,
longhaired tabby, constantly surprised me. She climbed up and over
everything. I had decorative curtains in our dining room that hung
low and made a loop much like hammock. Several times I found her
sleeping on her back inside those things. Not once did she become
tangled up in them—she just slid right out of them after her nap.

She walked on the inside edge of the fence and never missed
a beat. She jumped down from bathroom countertops and skidded
across a newly mopped floor. I came home one afternoon and found
her near the roofline of our raised ceiling on a thin beam. I don't
remember a time she didn't land on her feet. Even as she got older,
she remained highly responsive and swift on her feet. Sassy always
had a way of getting herself quickly in and out of situations.

Life has a way of turning things upside down and sideways,
especially when temptation comes. But the Lord always provides a
"way out" so we can stick the landing.

Lord, please give me the agility and balance I need always
to know which way is up when temptation turns my
world upside down. Help me to land on my feet.

My Defense

"The LORD is my strength and my defense;
he has become my salvation. He is my God, and I will
praise him, my father's God, and I will exalt him."

EXODUS 15:2 NIV

Our calico cat, Snickers, belonged to me—or should I say, I belonged to Snickers. Sometimes she rose up in jealousy when my husband approached. She'd nip at him or hiss. Usually she left him alone, but when it came to me, she rose up in fierce protection. I found it endearing, but of course my husband thought it annoying. Snickers was saying, "She's mine, not yours!"

The Bible identifies God as a jealous God. " 'Do not worship any other god, for the LORD, whose name is Jealous, is a jealous God' " (Exodus 34:14). Does that mean He's envious of what some people have and do? Not at all. It means He, like Snickers, rises up against the enemies of His people. However, He's not a harmless cat that can be shooed away.

Just like I found it heartwarming when Snickers fought for me, how much more meaningful is it that God rises up as our defender? When He sent Jesus to earth, it was His way of saying, "Satan, they're mine, not yours!"

Lord, thank You for buying me back from Satan with the
blood of Christ. I belong to You. In troublesome times,
remind me that You have my back.

Daddy's Home!

*Then all the people left, each for their own home, and David
returned home to bless his family.*

1 CHRONICLES 16:43 NIV

My cousin Phil explained his problem to me at a family reunion.
His daughter had brought a cat home from college, but she'd
recently moved for a job out of state. Her new apartment didn't
allow pets. Phil was taking care of his daughter's cat, but his wife
wasn't thrilled about this extra responsibility. The family dog hated
having competition and was protesting in the way only dogs can
protest.

"Can you take Cornelius?" he asked hopefully.

I shook my head, adamant. "My family said five cats is the
limit. They'll disown me if I bring another one in."

"Can you ask around?" Phil begged. "I don't know who else to ask."

I said I'd take the cat with the idea of looking for a forever
home for him. Phil told me to call the following Monday, and we'd
make arrangements to transfer the animal to my care. That next
week, I phoned just when Phil was returning home from work. He
answered the phone and said, "Hold on, Cornelius is rolling on his
back at my feet. I have to say hi to the cat first."

I knew right then that this pet transfer wouldn't go down. The
family managed to resolve their dog problem even while keeping
the cat.

Lord, give me clarity of mind so I can make
the right decisions that will benefit all
concerned. In Your name I pray, amen.

Two's Company. . .

Though one may be overpowered, two can defend themselves.
A cord of three strands is not quickly broken.

ECCLESIASTES 4:12 NIV

Things were peaceful in Terry's house with her dog, Willy, and cat, Kiska. Her two pets got along well. Then Terry brought a new puppy into the mix. Willy tires of little Sobaka's exuberance and endless energy. Sobaka frequently seeks a playmate, but Willy has better things to do—like sleep. So Sobaka looks for Kiska.

Sobaka has not learned yet that in Terry's house, dog and cat fights don't happen. When Sobaka tries to engage Kiska in a fight, Willy doesn't stand for it. He defends his longtime companion with a zeal surprising for an older dog.

A threesome, it's said, is a crowd. Not always so in the Bible. David's three mighty men defended their king and country with diligence (see 2 Samuel 23:8). Our system of government may be loosely based on Isaiah 33:22, where we're told "the LORD is our judge. . .lawgiver. . .[and] king." And finally, Jesus said, "For where two or three gather in my name, there am I with them" (Matthew 18:20).

Getting together with a couple of Christian friends? No dog or cat fights here! Enjoy your time together as Jesus blesses you with His presence.

Dear Lord, thank You for the time I can spend with friends who love You as I do. Thank You for joining us. Amen.

Bin Bad

Now He who searches the hearts knows what the
mind of the Spirit is, because He makes intercession
for the saints according to the will of God.
ROMANS 8:27 NKJV

My husband's sock and underwear bin in the laundry room has long been a spot where Bruce likes to curl up and take a nap. He fits perfectly in a ball on top of the warm, folded laundry. But when he had a case of fleas, we needed to rewash the laundry and turn the bin sideways toward the wall so he couldn't lie in it. He wasn't happy. A couple days later, I came home to find a stack of towels knocked to the floor along with the entire sock and underwear bin. Bruce was napping in the sideways bin with spilled laundry around him on the floor. He looked up at me as if to say, "You asked for this," and went right back to sleep.

After I thought about his comical rebellion, I realized I'm not a whole lot different. Sometimes God rearranges my life to protect me, and I am too unaware and untrusting of His plan. Then, I make a mess with complaints and misery that I wallow in for a while before I trust Him.

Lord, even in the hard changes You make in my life,
thank You that I can trust You and that
You constantly have me covered.

When Someone Dislikes Cats

*All things are lawful for me, but all things are not expedient:
all things are lawful for me, but all things edify not.*

1 CORINTHIANS 10:23 KJV

Believe it or not, there are some people who don't like cats for one reason or another. Many people have allergies that cause them to keep cats at a distance. Others have experienced something that left them traumatized by the presence of cats. Some folks are just dog lovers. Whatever the case, they would rather not be around anything feline in nature.

Personally, I'm quite glad to have our cat in our house. It would be very easy to have the attitude that it's our house, our cat, our rules. If you wish to come to my house, you'll have to accept my cat. I could rightfully have that expectation, but it wouldn't be very hospitable, and it might keep some from coming. For that reason, if we know we'll have guests who are bothered by our cat, we try to keep her out of sight.

In our Christian walk, we will come across things or behaviors that might not be wrong, but if we know it will cause a fellow Christian to stumble or an unbeliever to reject Christ, we should choose not to do those things to avoid being a stumbling block. It's worth the sacrifice if we can encourage someone to live for Christ.

Father, show me the things in my life that could
offend a fellow believer. Help me give them to You.

Rescued from the Dark

*For he has rescued us from the dominion of darkness
and brought us into the kingdom of the Son he loves,
in whom we have redemption, the forgiveness of sins.*
COLOSSIANS 1:13–14 NIV

Oliver, a silver-gray male, wasn't quite a year old when he went missing. Brady allowed Oliver to go out, but he always came back before dark. As night began to fall, Brady called Oliver to come home. Clouds rolled in, and heavy drops of rain signaled a big storm just minutes out.

Then Brady heard him. He followed the sound of Oliver's cries for help and located him twenty or thirty feet up the neighbor's tree. Time was short. Brady ran into the house to grab his phone and flashlight.

He dialed 911 and called for rescue as the cool, damp night surrounded them. Minutes later, the fire truck pulled up next to the house. Heavy rain began to fall as Brady stood helpless, thankful for the rescue team as he watched them work to reach Oliver.

Brady let the air he'd been holding in escape his lips, relieved to see Oliver as the firemen passed him gently down the ladder. Oliver, frightened and wet, hid his head in Brady's jacket, thankful to be in safe in Brady's arms.

Lord, sometimes I find myself in dark or difficult places.
Thank You for Your promise to always be with me.
I am grateful for the many times You reached in
and rescued me from the dark.

Little Things

*Just as a body, though one, has many parts, but all
its many parts form one body, so it is with Christ.*

1 CORINTHIANS 12:12 NIV

For over sixteen years, our calico cat, Snickers, had been a special
friend to me. One day as I petted her, I felt a lump. I took her to the
vet. To have it removed would be costly, and the surgery was not
guaranteed to lengthen her life. So I brought her home until it became
problematic. Finally, I took Snickers for her last trip to the vet.

Weeks later, my husband and I were putting supper away when
I dropped some salmon on the floor. Loren and I looked at each
other and said, "No cat!" Even though Snickers took more from our
relationship than she gave, she did make her contributions.
I cleaned up the mess, missing her.

We each have a part in the body of Christ, no matter how
miniscule it seems. In fact, 1 Corinthians 12:22 says, "Those parts
of the body that seem to be weaker are indispensable." A good
question to ask ourselves is "What part can I play in the body of
Christ today?" If God impresses on us to reach out to someone in a
small way, we mustn't disregard it as insignificant. Sometimes, it's
the little things, such as a word of encouragement, that a person
needs the most.

Father, help me be faithful to do my part,
regardless of how unimportant it seems.

Cookie Crumbles

"Nevertheless the LORD your God would not listen to Balaam,
but the LORD your God turned the curse into a blessing
for you, because the LORD your God loves you."
DEUTERONOMY 23:5 NKJV

Glistening with candies and spice drops, the gingerbread house sat on the counter for our kitchen's adornment over Christmas break. My son Dexter and his friends enjoyed hours together assembling it and painstakingly decorating it to perfection.

The next morning a little piece came up missing and a few crumbles sat next to the Chiclet sidewalk. Dexter told me with a little frowning smirk that he suspected Dad had taken a piece of candy off the roofline, but Dad was not home to defend himself.

The next morning, a little chunk of cookie on the back of the house came up missing and a bigger mess was left behind. "Mom, seriously! I think Dad is eating the gingerbread."

The morning after that, Dad was home. He was making coffee when Dexter and I came into the kitchen. "Hey," my husband said, "I caught Jak on the counter again in the middle of the night messing with the gingerbread house."

Sometimes a situation is turned right on its head. We all had a good laugh together! It was a great reminder to me to seek understanding before jumping to conclusions and that often things are not at all as they may appear.

God, give me an open heart and mind for others
and for the situations that may frustrate me today.
I can trust You to make a blessing out of something
that seems quite the opposite.

Morning Song

But I will sing of your strength, in the morning I will sing of your love; for you are my fortress, my refuge in times of trouble.

PSALM 59:16 NIV

Lori loves the early morning. She enjoys sitting on her back porch with coffee and her Bible, savoring the quiet and watching the sunrise. She even likes to sing quiet songs of praise.

Unfortunately, her cat, Sadie, likes to join in by singing the song of her people. Her loud, off-key mewing doesn't contribute to the serenity Lori longs for. Sometimes Lori will stomp her foot to try and shush Sadie. She's even been known to use her foot to gently move Sadie back into the house.

But after all that, the mood is usually gone. As Lori shared this story with me, she said, "The moral is: it's hard to worship God after you've kicked the cat."

We laugh, but it's true. We often think that in order to truly praise God, the circumstances have to be perfect. But God wants us to praise Him in the middle of chaos. In the center of storms. In the cacophony of cat songs. Perhaps that kind of praise is even more beautiful to God's ears than our sweet songs of serenity.

Dear Father, help me to praise You in the quiet and in the chaos, in the easy times and the difficult times. Remind me that Your peace is mine at all times; I just have to choose to take it.

A Member of the Family

God sets the lonely in families.
PSALM 68:6 NIV

Their discovery was not a happy one.

Paul and Sharon went to their lake cottage to find a cat and seven kittens snuggled under their porch. Sharon and her husband (who have never had pets) went about finding families to take in the brood of kittens. They had no trouble finding homes for the litter. The mother cat was another story. A kitten was one thing; a grown cat was something else. No one wanted the cat they nicknamed "Willa."

The couple took a liking to their little squatter and took Willa in as their own. The former homeless cat enjoys life as a pampered *indoor* cat now.

Many people have no family connection. Relocation, separation, death—all leave individuals isolated, without family. One couple we know reaches out to singles. Frequently they invite a single woman or an elderly widower to join them and their family for a meal—to share in "family" more than food. In our church, a number of families "adopt" international university students to provide them with connection. Many of those students have younger siblings at home whom they miss. The children of their US families give them a delight they lack with dormitory friends and classmates.

How like our loving God who orchestrates it all! As David wrote in another psalm, "This poor man called, and the LORD heard him" (Psalm 34:6).

Lord, never allow me to overlook the lonely.

Unexpected Adoption

For ye have not received the spirit of bondage again to fear; but ye have received the Spirit of adoption, whereby we cry, Abba, Father.
ROMANS 8:15 KJV

The pastor announced that one of our members had found a sweet little kitten, and, due to allergies, she was unable to keep it. She wondered if anyone in the church would want it. I elbowed my husband, and he knew that before the evening ended we would have a new pet.

We arrived at the woman's house, and she brought the kitten out. Only he wasn't a kitten. He was a full-grown tom. We started laughing when we realized this. In her eyes he really was a kitten, but we'd been around a few more cats than she had. She was afraid we wouldn't want him since he wasn't as small as we'd expected, but we decided we'd keep him anyway, so Jeb made the trip home with us that night.

I'm afraid sometimes we're guilty of looking at people and thinking there's no reason to try to win them to Christ. We figure they won't be interested or that somehow they're less deserving of Christ's salvation than we are. The truth is that God wants all of us to be part of His family. He will gladly make all who come to Him His sons and daughters. No longer slaves to sin, the adopted child of God becomes joint-heir with Jesus.

Thank You, God, for adopting me into Your family.

Big Green Machine and Fear

They will have no fear of bad news;
their hearts are steadfast, trusting in the LORD.
PSALM 112:7 NIV

Filbert is the only one of my cats who loves the garbage truck. The others run and hide. Old Filbert jumps on my lap to share the experience with me. I'm usually sitting at the window, typing on my laptop, when the garbage truck turns onto our street. My boy feels safer with me than in hiding behind the sofa. Together we make a big deal out of the arrival of the Big Green Garbage Machine.

"It's here," I coo to Filbert. "Come protect Mommy." He snuggles close but sticks his head up to stare out the window. The truck clunks past our driveway and stops.

"You watch those guys," I tell Filbert. "This is our house. They're on our driveway." He watches intently while the workers trudge across our concrete to grab the bags I put out before dawn. *Thump, thump* echoes up to our window as the men toss those bags in the back of their truck. The compactor inside chews them up. Filbert is loving it. Any kind of noise grabs his attention. He stares down this potential menace with all his might, as if by doing so, he's on top on things, in total control, my own Mister Fearless.

Lord, help us to empathize with our pets when situations occur that are fearful to them. Just as we trust in You, Lord, help us to be a secure presence to them.

Has God Spoken to You?

The heavens declare the glory of God; the skies proclaim the work of his hands. Day after day they pour forth speech.

PSALM 19:1–2 NIV

Lori and her cat, Belle, talk to one another. Lori's husband doubts this, of course, but Lori says she can tell the difference between Belle's "yes" and "no" meows. They have two different timbres and sounds. After eighteen years, Lori does recognize dear old Belle's "yes" from her "no."

God's Word, the Bible, tells us that we have all heard the voice of God whether we recognize it or not. Even though the heavens and skies "have no speech. . .use no words [and] no sound is heard from them. . . their voice goes out into all the earth" (Psalm 19:3, 4). Romans restates this truth in no uncertain terms. "What may be known about God is plain to [people], because God has made it plain to them" (Romans 1:19).

We read the same sentiment, conveyed with more intimacy than in the Romans verse, in the book of Hebrews. "In the past God spoke to our ancestors through the prophets at many times and in various ways, but in these last days he has spoken to us by his Son" (Hebrews 1:1–2).

Waiting for a word from God? He *has* spoken; His last and best word to us is in His Son, the Lord Jesus Christ.

Lord, give me ears to hear Your voice above all others. Amen.

Mama Kitty

"Therefore go and make disciples of all nations, baptizing them in the name of the Father and of the Son and of the Holy Spirit, and teaching them to obey everything I have commanded you."

MATTHEW 28:19–20 NIV

Mama Kitty was fat and sweet and lazy, and she wouldn't hurt a fly. Or a mouse. Rick thought her lack of hunting prowess was due to lack of opportunity since she stayed indoors and was fed a king's banquet every day.

But one day, a mouse showed up in the house! It ran in the bathroom, so Rick quickly shut the door. He got Mama Kitty and took her in the bathroom, and he perched himself on the counter to watch the show. Only, there was no show.

Mama Kitty noticed the mouse, purred a friendly hello, and promptly laid down and went to sleep. She had no interest in harming that little creature. That would be too much work. Rick had to catch the mouse himself.

In the Western world, it's easy to become spoiled by our brand of Christianity. We go to our fancy church buildings, show up for coffee or tea at a ladies' meeting, and enjoy our comfortable lives. But we were made for more.

When we fail to live out our purpose—to go into the world and share Christ's love with all people—we become spiritually fat and lazy. And we never experience the thrill of living out our true purpose as children of God.

Dear Father, forgive me for being lazy about my purpose. Give me opportunities to share Your love with people who don't know You.

Actual Rescue Cat

Stretch out Your hand from above; rescue me and deliver me out of great waters, from the hand of foreigners.

PSALM 144: 7 NKJV

The day before Thanksgiving break, I received a call at work from my son, Mitch. "Mom, I hope you don't mind, but I found a tiny kitten. She's kind of beat up, and she's in the garage. Maybe you can help me with her."

When I got home, the cutest little gray striped kitten was happy to see me. Not only did she have matted eyes but a part of her back paw pad had been severed. At not even six weeks old—and found a long way from any homes—she'd clearly been discarded along the roadside. We doctored her with a warm sponge bath, eye salve, and disinfectant cream. In just two days she was looking healthy and rambunctious. We named her Katniss, and later, Mr. Katniss. Oops!

Every day Mr. Katniss is happy to see us, his rescuers. All because Mitch saw something move in the field that caused him to stop on his way through. The little kitten surely would have died of exposure that night in his weak state. I found myself so proud of my kindhearted son who, reflecting the love of his heavenly Father, couldn't stand to see a creature suffer or go uncared for.

Lord, thank You for being just like this for me,
seeing my desperate state, meeting my needs,
and loving me right where You find me.

Claim Your Space

*"Every place on which the sole
of your foot treads shall be yours."*
DEUTERONOMY 11:24 NKJV

A sleek black cat claimed our house as home. We didn't bring her inside, but we fed her scraps and she thrived, even gaining some weight.

Our vacation took us away for two weeks, and we figured she wouldn't be there when we returned. But we barely opened the garage door when she greeted us. She still looked healthy. Someone must have taken our place caring for her.

One day she didn't show up, and the kids and I were disappointed. That night was rainy and cool, but we figured she was safe in a comfy shelter. At bedtime, though, we heard a sorrowful meow somewhere outside. After a brief investigation, we discovered her in a window well—along with five tiny kittens.

Even my non-cat-loving husband couldn't refuse hospitality for a new mother on a cold night. Using some old blankets, we turned a box into a cozy nest for her family in our garage. The next morning, our children raced downstairs to make sure everyone was okay, but the box was empty, so another search began. Our basement was just off the garage, and it didn't take long to find where she'd moved. We had an old bassinet (complete with bedding) stored downstairs, and she decided that was a much more acceptable nursery.

Father, let me claim my safe place in You,
the one who always provides for all my needs.

The Elusive Fox

And Jesus saith unto him, The foxes have holes, and the birds of the air have nests; but the Son of man hath not where to lay his head.
MATTHEW 8:20 KJV

Fox is a wanderer. We'll see him, then he'll be gone for weeks, even months at a time. Just when we've forgotten about him, he'll reappear. We don't know where he's been or what he's been through, but evidently the lifestyle satisfies him, and when he does return, he's no worse for the wear. We don't know where he came from or if he belongs to anyone. He keeps to himself, and when he's through with whatever has brought him here, he leaves.

Jesus moved from place to place, too. There was a man who came to him and boasted that he would follow Jesus wherever He went. Immediately Jesus told the man it would be no life of ease. "I don't even have a place to call my own," Jesus told him. Jesus wasn't complaining, but He wanted the man to understand that he'd have to make some sacrifices if he truly planned to follow Christ.

We don't know what complete surrender to Christ will entail. He doesn't ask us to know up front or to have it all planned out. He only asks us to trust Him. When we can do that, then we'll know we're truly available to Him.

I want to follow You at any cost, dear Lord.

Comfort from a Friend

Be kindly affectionate to one another with brotherly love,
in honor giving preference to one another.
ROMANS 12:10 NKJV

Donna and her family had a Maltese-Shih Tzu mix named Sassy and
a stray cat that she rescued when he was about four weeks old who
came to be known as Sam. Sassy and Sam grew up together. They
were the best of friends.

At seven years old, Sassy had never had puppies. Donna
assumed she couldn't get pregnant, so the whole family was
surprised when she had her first litter. Sadly, only two of Sassy's
puppies survived, and Donna found homes for them.

Sassy grieved deeply for her puppies, and her best friend, Sam,
tried to comfort her. Sassy looked everywhere for the puppies. It
hurt Donna's heart, too, and her parents decided there would be no
more puppies for Sassy. It was just too sad.

One afternoon, Donna's mom looked out the kitchen window
and saw the cat, Sam, coming over the fence with a puppy in his
mouth. He put the puppy in Sassy's bed. It was as if he had gone
on a mission to bring Sassy's baby back to her and had finally
succeeded. Donna's heart melted as she realized just how much
these two loved each other.

Heavenly Father, thank You for the relationships
You have given me. You've reached out and comforted
me within the loving arms of those I know and love.
Help me to recognize those opportunities to
share Your love with others.

A Joyful Noise

Make a joyful noise unto the LORD, all ye lands. Serve the
LORD with gladness: come before his presence with singing.
PSALM 100:1–2 KJV

When my kids were little, they used to sing a cute song at preschool,
"All God's creatures have a place in the choir, / Some sing low, some
sing higher, / Some sing out loud on a telephone wire, / Some just
clap their hands, or paws, or anything they've got now."

Once, when I stayed at my sister's house, I heard mysterious
piano sounds coming from the living room in the middle of the
night. It wasn't a beautiful song wafting through the air, but random
notes, *plunk, plunk, plunk.* In the morning, I asked my sister about
it. It wasn't a ghost, but Sy, her gray cat. For some reason when the
house was quiet, the cat liked to put on a concert, walking up and
down the keyboard. She had a place in God's orchestra.

Sometimes we may be so focused on our daily to-dos that
we forget about our wondrous Creator. The great news is that He
desires to fellowship with His people. Remember to sing a song of
praise and thanksgiving to the Lord—even if it may only qualify as a
joyful—rather than skillful—noise, or if it has to wait until the middle
of the night, like Sy.

Holy God, Three in One, my heart sings to You in worship,
for You are good and worthy to be praised.

Bruce and the Shoulder Transfer

"Look at the birds of the air, for they neither sow nor reap
nor gather into barns; yet your heavenly Father feeds them.
Are you not of more value than they?"
MATTHEW 6:26 NKJV

Who can understand the allure of a shoulder to this cat? Not me. But Bruce loves to be held over a shoulder. Any shoulder. If he's in the vicinity of your shoulder, he will request to hop aboard. A pause is all he needs as a yes. It does not matter which shoulder, right or left, or where you are—in the garden, on the floor, at the garage workbench, or sitting on the couch. He would love to rest over your shoulder anytime, anywhere.

When I think about it, who doesn't like the warmth of another? The comfort of the human touch. The vantage point from up above your usual view.

So, there are days that I go to work with cat hair on my neck. This shoulder love is not exactly convenient, but it's totally worth it. And when I think about how God cares for His creatures every moment of every day, the cats and, even more so, me—I am in awe of His greatness.

God, thank You for the blessing of caring
for Your creation through my pets and the
joy of being so loved by them and You.

The Quality of Life

*"Say to him: 'Long life to you! Good health to you and
your household! And good health to all that is yours!'"*

1 SAMUEL 25:6 NIV

Good health—this is the number one concern of people everywhere.
All living creatures, humans and animals alike, want to live free
from pain. That's why I pray for the blessings of good health for all
my family members, friends, and even my pets.

Our five cats are cherished members of our household. I
remember them in my prayers by name. I thank the Lord for
entrusting them to my care. I ask the Lord to look kindly upon
them, keep them from accidents, and make me, as their human
companion, always mindful of their needs. We know that God is
with us during each step of our daily walk, just as we are there for
our pets. They look to us as their guiding light.

Moxie, our American shorthair, is showing her age. The vet
told us this is the "new normal" for her. She still radiates the joy of
life. We do what we can to make her life easier. We can't help every
animal in the world, but we can help this one. This is the girl that
God put in our path, so we're on the road of life together, wherever
it may lead us.

Lord, help us to continue the tradition of ancient Bible times,
where man and woman were given dominion over the animals
of the earth with the responsibility to keep them safe.

Obedient When It Suits Me

*Saul and his men spared Agag's life and kept the best of
the sheep and. . .cattle, the fat calves, and the lambs—
everything, in fact, that appealed to them.*

1 SAMUEL 15:9 NLT

Amy, our cat, always walked with the kids. When Halloween
came around, she decided she should go trick-or-treating to every
house right along with her young charges. Chris, the mom of the
household, decided this wasn't such a good idea with so many other
children about, so she gave a solitary command to Amy: "Go home!"
Amy obeyed—or so Chris thought.

When she and the children made it around the block and were
returning home, surprise! Amy jumped out from behind the bush
where she had been patiently waiting. It was then she obeyed and
went home—right alongside the children.

Have any of your children or pets ever done this to you?
Followed your directions at their leisure? Obeyed you halfway?
Maybe your son procrastinates when it's time to take out the
trash. Or your cat doesn't stay off the table like you instructed.
Frustrating? Yes. Like my obedience to God sometimes? Possibly. . .
maybe even probably.

Saul's biggest problem was only being obedient when it suited
him. The Lord thought little of it millennia ago, and He hasn't changed
His mind. "Obedience is better than sacrifice" (1 Samuel 15:22).

Holy Spirit, help me to be an
obedient child of the King. Amen.

Another Comforter

And I will pray the Father, and he shall give you
another Comforter, that he may abide with you for ever.

JOHN 14:16 KJV

The loss of a pet is never an easy thing, and though my sweet girl tried to be brave when her kitten died, she was really quite devastated. It took some time for the hurt to begin healing, but eventually it did. She found comfort in the playful, cuddly antics of a fun-loving new kitten, Bubble. They were soon best buddies, and while she never forgot her Daisy, she had happiness with Bubble.

There is a lot of unrest in this world. It was true even at the time Jesus lived on earth. He knew His time here was limited, so He began to prepare His disciples for the time He would no longer physically be with them. They didn't want to be without Him and probably wondered how they would ever manage, but He promised that He would send the Holy Spirit, their new Comforter, who would be with them.

It's impossible to find true and enduring peace in a world corrupted by sin. There is hurt. There is evil and misunderstanding, but praise God—believers can have peace that passes all understanding! The Holy Spirit still works in the lives of believers: teaching us, revealing God's truth to us, and enveloping us in peace and love.

Thank You, Jesus, for sending me a Comforter.

Rescue Cat

He delivers and rescues, and He works signs and wonders in heaven and on earth, who has delivered Daniel from the power of the lions.
DANIEL 6:27 NKJV

I don't completely know what made Eva such a timid cat. But she is a gray and white fluff ball of sensitivity and has squeaked since we brought her home. I had to give her a little more grace after she birthed six kittens and was more sensitive than ever. Still, we've had plenty of litters come through our little farm, and no mama kitty ever had the issues Eva did. Her apparent spikes in estrogen brought complex behavior, sometimes extreme. She became aggressive with the other cats and despondent even with her own kittens. At times, she took just two of the six to a safe place and left the others behind as if to say, "I just want two, thank you."

Previously well trained, she would rebelliously make a puddle on the rug and stare right at me. For this, she was swatted and brought to the litter box, with no improvement. She even had to live outside for a time, which seemed to help a great deal.

Fast forward a few years to my son's friend visiting us. He noticed Eva's timidity when he tried to pet her. "Is she a rescue cat?" he asked.

"No." I said a bit sternly.

"Does she need to be?"

My son and I erupted with laughter before giving a little Eva history lesson.

Lord God, in my complexities, which can be extreme in their own way, thank You that You are always present and working on my rescue.

Bad Judgment Calls

*If any of you lacks wisdom, you should
ask God . . . and it will be given to you.*

JAMES 1:5 NIV

Sarah, a blue Persian with more energy than sense, decided to leap from the sofa to the recliner. In midflight she figured out she had misjudged the distance. The realization played out clearly on her whiskered puss. *Uh-oh. . .*

Wham! She hit the back of the chair headfirst. Being a cat, she didn't dwell on her error. She continued to make a few more bad calls—like the night she tried to climb the Christmas tree.

I was in the back of my upstairs apartment when I heard the crash. My neighbors downstairs came bolting up the steps, expecting to find me dead on the floor. The Christmas tree—less some now-shattered ornaments—lay on the carpet. Sarah sat looking at us from a corner.

She conjured innocence on that same whiskered puss—now sporting some pine needles. "Me? I was sitting here minding my own business!"

My judgment calls have little to do with judging distances or climbing Christmas trees. Mine are more serious. Should I allow my daughter to go to that party? Should we take that financial risk to move into a bigger house?

When hard choices confront us, God encourages us to seek Him for the wisdom we need. "The LORD gives wisdom; from his mouth come knowledge and understanding" (Proverbs 2:6).

Father, please help me to judge wisely today. Amen.

Church Cat

I will strengthen thee; yea, I will help thee; yea,
I will uphold thee with the right hand of my righteousness.
ISAIAH 41:10 KJV

A local pastor told the story of how every week he'd walk into the sanctuary of their church and pray over each seat. One day as he prayed, a flash of fur rushed past him, and he was shocked out of his prayer time. He followed the mysterious blaze to discover a little cat that had somehow gotten into the building.

The pastor began to leave food and water for his new friend, and soon he was known as Buster, the church cat. Everyone in the congregation claimed him as their own. But one day, Buster went missing.

People searched high and low. They left food on the church steps, but it went untouched. They drove through the neighborhood, calling, but to no avail.

Several days passed, and one of the church members noticed the blinds in one of the storage rooms had fallen to the ground. Sure enough, when they entered the room, there was Buster on top of a cardboard box. He was hungry and thirsty, and quite relieved to be released from his prison.

Sometimes we find ourselves trapped in prisons of anger, bitterness, sadness, guilt, or anything else that may keep us from moving forward. But there is one who searches for us. God will stop at nothing to rescue us from the circumstances that would harm us. If we'll call out to Him, He will find us, offer us refreshment, and care for us.

Dear Father, help me let go of things that
keep me trapped. I need You to rescue me.

119

Something's in Our Shed

*I can lie down and sleep soundly because you,
LORD, will keep me safe.*

PSALM 4:8 CEV

"Something's living in our shed," my husband, Jake, said after he put away the lawnmower out back. "I stepped on a dead mouse going in."

"Some cat looking for warmth," I guessed. "Nights are getting colder. Those boards are loose."

Jake said he saw a flash of orange dash out when he left the door open. A ginger cat, it looked like. We wondered if it would come back. It did, the next evening at dusk. It was fatter than the usual stray. I wondered if it was lost or just roaming.

"I can put some food out," I volunteered, "but I don't want to encourage it if another family's looking for it."

"Look at them hawks flying above Industrial Boulevard," Jake said the next day as we watched from our glider. A red-tailed hawk flew in the distance above the trees near the storage barns on the hill. "You think I should leave the door open? Keep that cat safe?"

"For now. I'll check online about lost cats." We put out cheap cat food to help our visitor keep up its strength. The cat was gone in a week. Maybe it found a pack of strays to live with. We never saw the cat again, but we were glad that we were able to give it safety and rest in a dangerous place.

Keep us safe within your care, O Lord, we humbly pray.
Just as we need a safe place to lay down our
head at night, so do our animal friends.

Attention! Attention!

"Still other seed fell on good soil. It came up and yielded a crop,
a hundred times more than was sown." When he said this,
he called out, "Whoever has ears to hear, let them hear."
LUKE 8:8 NIV

Cats have a way of getting their human's attention, whether it's persistent meowing or continual hovering. My daughter's cats, Kit Kat and Kaboodle, have their ways, too. Kaboodle flops before her feet. Perhaps she's trying to trip her to get her to cat level. Kit Kat is even more aggressive. He discovered a way to get people hopping— by nipping their toes!

God has a way of getting our attention, too. On our better days it's that still, small voice, the Holy Spirit, saying, "This is the way, walk in it." Sometimes it's repetition in His Word, like the admonition "Be strong and courageous," which is in the Bible hundreds of times. Or sometimes it's a repetition in your life. Do you ever keep running into the same person all of the time? And sometimes He whaps you upside the head by allowing some kind of hardship.

Let's not make it difficult for God to get our attention. We need to spend time in His Word, in prayer, and with other believers. A soft meow is much more pleasant than a bite on the toes.

Lord, open my ears to Your will and ways. May I respond
today in love to whomever You put in my path.

The Right Focus

Let us run with perseverance the race marked out for us,
fixing our eyes on Jesus, the pioneer and protector of faith.
HEBREWS 12:1-2 NIV

When my sons were little, they enjoyed the shows on Animal Planet and would often watch them at Meemaw's house. Even after the boys went home, Meemaw left the television on the Animal Planet station for the noise as she worked around the house.

One of the shows about cats had a specific jingle for the introduction, and Meemaw noticed her cat, Molly, sitting in front of the television. Molly seemed to like this show. Intrigued, Meemaw began to observe Molly. Meemaw realized that no matter where Molly was in the house, when she heard the music for the introduction of the cat show she liked, she would run into the living room, sit down, and give the show her full attention. Once in a while, she would even reach out with her paw and try to touch the cats on the screen. Surprisingly, as soon as the show was over, Molly would leave the room.

Lord, what I give my attention to is important. Time spent with You in prayer, in Your Word, and with other believers must be a priority. Today I give You my full attention during my time with You. Help me listen for You as You speak to me today. Amen.

A Daring Rescue

What man of you, having an hundred sheep, if he lose one of them,
doth not leave the ninety and nine in the wilderness,
and go after that which is lost, until he find it?

LUKE 15:4 KJV

Several cats were milling about on the porch, but the kittens were missing. We could hear them mewing, and they sounded distressed, but we just weren't sure where they were. As we listened, we realized it was coming from the pole building nearby. The kids headed in that direction, determined to find their absent pets and bring them home.

Once they got there, it was easy to figure out where the kittens were, but retrieving them would require creativity and a certain amount of acrobatics. It was obvious that the cat who had stolen them from their mama didn't want them rescued, but after a bit of twisting and turning and putting herself into precarious positions, my daughter pulled them from their prison and restored them to their rightful mother.

Jesus did that for us. He said we are His sheep, and He protects us as a shepherd should. How often we go astray, but thank God for His mercy! When we wander, He doesn't give us up automatically. He comes after us, even into the worst possible situations, to draw us back to Himself. What a joy to be drawn close in His loving arms!

Your mercy is beyond compare.
You truly are my Good Shepherd.

Basic Training

Start children off on the way they should go,
and even when they are old they will not turn from it.
PROVERBS 22:6 NIV

Watching our mother cat train her little ones, beginning when they were tiny, was great fun. Humans could benefit from some of her teaching philosophy.

Lucy apparently didn't believe she should spare the rod. Not that she used a rod, but she did bop her babies on their rumps with her paw when they misbehaved. Then she snuggled them close.

Sometimes the kittens' play got a little rough. That didn't bother Momma, even if one cried out occasionally. She relaxed in a corner and watched them have fun, blinking once in a while. She was probably delighted that they weren't pestering her for food.

Lucy even encouraged social involvement. If one of the babies strayed away from its siblings or appeared standoffish, she picked it up and dropped it back into the furry heap of the others. Sometimes she tossed a fuzzy toy in the air and intercepted it before the kittens could, like showing them how to play keep-away.

As they grew, she seemed to work on survival skills. She would crouch, her tail moving slowly back and forth, eyeing some imaginary prey before she pounced to capture it. The kittens followed her leadership. They crouched and pounced—on one another—then tumbled together.

Dear Lord, we all need a good teacher.
Continue showing me Your way, and let my life be
an example to teach others the joy of living for You.

The Big Freak Out

*For if our heart condemns us, God is greater
than our heart, and knows all things.*

1 JOHN 3:20 NKJV

If you have multiple cats, you understand the tricky dynamics of the cat community in your home. They vie for position, mark their places, often need their own litter boxes, and get along in unique relationships. It's not entirely different from humans, I suppose.

So, indulge me as I share a bit of cat drama. We had three cats at the time, and a black and white stray kept impregnating Zelda. We suspected that Eva, now nearing a year old, was also pregnant. On a dark winter night, our alpha cat, Bruce, began growling as he looked out the french door. He spotted the black and white stray out on the deck. Eva inched in sheepishly for a peek outside. Bruce's protest became louder as he looked at Eva. Then he stared straight at her and began shrieking unlike anything I've ever heard. Eva shrieked back. It was a shriek fest! One son ran up from the basement, and another ran down from upstairs to investigate. We were pretty sure that Bruce just realized Eva was pregnant by the stray. "I never thought cats had drama until now," my son, Trevor, said.

God, thank You that nothing is a surprise to You and for
loving me no matter what kind of chaos I find myself in.

Out of Sight

Don't let the sun go down while you are still angry.
EPHESIANS 4:26 NLT

Jeri and Ron live next to a meadow. Their house, convenient for any cold mice that may be afield, serves as a nice warming hut. One wintery day, however, a mouse got into their home between the drywall and the exterior brick. The mouse could be heard scuttling back and forth and up and down, but Jeri wasn't about to put a hole in the wall to rid the house of the critter.

And the cats? Out of sight is out of mind.

The desperate rodent ate his way around a bathroom light fixture. He landed in the sink bowl from which all the scuttling in the world couldn't free him. Ron had to catch him while the cats contentedly napped.

Out of sight is, after all, out of mind.

When someone has hurt me, or I know I need to ask someone's forgiveness, it can be easy to overlook it if it's not a problem *today*—or if I don't have contact with that person *today*. God says we need to deal with such things quickly—no matter who is at fault (see Matthew 5:23-24). "Out of sight, out of mind" does not work before God—just like Ron couldn't wait until the cats had a mind to do something about that mouse!

Lord, I pray to deal with painful
relationships in Your way and Your time.

Rest Easy

Return to your rest, my son, for the LORD has been good to you.
PSALM 116:7 NKJV

The day we adopted our kitten, Black Purrl, we brought home a great deal of accoutrements. Litter box and food bowl, collar and leash, kitty treats and wand toys—we went crazy buying her "cute" this and "sweet" that. We also bought a "cat condo" with a sleeping space, a scratching post, and jingly plastic balls suspended from the corners.

She rarely uses the scratching post, entirely ignores the balls, and never sleeps in the bed. Where does she sleep? The lounge chair. The dogs' bed. Our bed. Inside one of Craig's size-fifteen tennis shoes. She has napped in a tissue box, the bottom drawer of the filing cabinet, atop a pile of warm, clean clothing, and in my gardening hat—in short, anywhere but her bed. While I am puzzled by her choice of sleeping locations, I do envy her ability to take a nap anywhere she chooses.

I always intend to get a good night's sleep, but. . .I have e-mails to return, chores to do, and decisions to make. Night by night, my rest is eaten away by the exigencies of the day and the worries of tomorrow. Perhaps it's time to take a lesson from Black Purrl. God knows what happened today and already holds tomorrow. I can rest secure in His protection.

Lord Jesus, I choose to rest in You today.

Bogey

*No discipline seems pleasant at the time, but painful.
Later on, however, it produces a harvest of righteousness
and peace for those who have been trained by it.*

HEBREWS 12:11 NIV

Bogey was a big cat. Enormous. And strong! Bogey wasn't fat. . .he was all muscle.

Fortunately, he was good natured and loving. And fortunately, his owners had the foresight to have him declawed, because every once in a while, Bogey lost his temper.

Oh, he didn't hiss and scratch. Bogey was too cool for that. Instead, he'd sit quietly, tolerating whatever behavior annoyed him, with a snooty air that said, "I wish you'd stop. Until you do, I'll ignore you." But after a time, Bogey would have enough and *WHAP!* He'd slap that mammoth paw once in your direction, and sometimes, he'd leave a bruise.

Then he'd meow sweetly, as if to say he was sorry for hurting you, but he didn't have any other choice. Then he'd cuddle up and offer his eternal love. At least until next time.

In some ways, Bogey was kind of like God. Enormous. Strong. And extremely long-suffering. But long-suffering doesn't mean forever-suffering. When we act in rebellion toward God, He gives us every opportunity to repent. He lets us know we're doing wrong and waits patiently for us to stop. But there comes a point when *WHAP.* God's discipline comes roaring down, and sometimes, it leaves a bruise.

But soon God reaches out to us again, reminding us that He wants to be near us, wrapping His great arms around us in a show of eternal love.

Dear Father, thank You for Your discipline. Help me to
submit to Your will before Your patience wears out.

Growing Cats

For when for the time ye ought to be teachers, ye have need that one
teach you again which be the first principles of the oracles of God;
and are become such as have need of milk, and not of strong meat.

HEBREWS 5:12 KJV

The cats used to be happy to get a dishful of milk, but somewhere
along the line, someone began slipping them scraps and leftovers.
It didn't take them long to figure out the pattern. Humans prepare
the meals. Humans eat the meals. Humans clean up the meals.
Cats receive goodies. They obviously looked forward to it because
they would sit outside the kitchen door waiting expectantly.
Occasionally one would stand on its hind legs and peer in as we ate.

Then they became bossy. They would no sooner hear plates
being scraped than they would leap onto the screen door and meow
demandingly. They wanted the good stuff, and they were going
after it. Sometimes when the door would open, they would dart into
the house and begin eating whatever the little ones had dropped.
Whatever was necessary, it was worth it to them to get those leftovers.

Why aren't we more like that as Christians? For new believers,
the milk of God's Word is necessary, but so many people get stuck
there. In order for us to make a difference for Jesus, we're going to
have to go after the meatier things in scripture. We need them to
grow!

Dear God, fill me with the meat of Your Word!

The Eyes Have It

*Then Jesus told his disciples a parable to show
them that they should always pray and not give up.*
LUKE 18:1 NIV

My friend's four cats are Charlotte, Chester, Bonnie, and Frank Sinatra. They generally ignore me when I visit, but one particular day, curiosity got the best of Frank, and he leaped up on my lap. Frank is a longhaired cream-colored cat, fifteen pounds and twenty-one inches long from nose to rump. He stood on my lap and put his front paws on my shoulders and looked into my eyes with his very blue ones. There was no ignoring this cat, so I stroked his fur and spoke affectionately to him.

Jesus tells the story about a woman who persistently pled her case before an unjust judge. Finally the judge grew weary of her continual coming and granted her request. After the parable, Jesus asked (in essence), "If an unjust judge would respond to the widow, how much more will God answer our persistent prayers?"

Hebrews 4:16 says to come boldly to the throne of grace. Sometimes we have to take on the audacity of Frank Sinatra the cat. Spiritually speaking, we climb up on Daddy's lap, put our hands on His shoulders, and look into His eyes and make our wants and wishes known.

Father, thank You that You do hear our prayers.
Work in my heart that I might have the persistence
and boldness to receive whatever You have for me.

Drooling Desire

May He grant you according to your heart's desire,
and fulfill all your purpose.
PSALM 20:4 NKJV

Mr. Katniss is an outdoor cat on the farm. So when he has the opportunity to hang out with me on the porch, he is so happy. He rubs his face on my ankles and hops up on the seat to try to get a spot on my lap. He often drools when I pet him. Now, I have seen animals drool for many kinds of food, water, or even toys. But I have wondered, *Could a cat care that much about getting a bit of attention for a few minutes?* Apparently, yes.

In a way, when I think about how great my desires are, I can sort of get it. How I desire daily to connect with others in a positive way, to encourage my family, and to maintain or mend relationships. So it's not too hard to understand my cat, I guess. I just usually skip the drooling part!

Lord, thank You that You truly know my heart's desire and give me a purpose to fulfill. You are so good to me!

A Rare Male Tortie

Gold there is, and rubies in abundance,
but lips that speak knowledge are a rare jewel.
PROVERBS 20:15 NIV

My neighbor was telling us she'd taken in a tortie cat that was hanging around her garage. I asked, "I've heard of a puddy cat. What's a tortie cat?"

"It's short for 'tortoise shell,'" she explained, meaning Nelda had patches of orange and gold coloring all over her black body, just like a tortoise or turtle has patches on its shell. She was sure it was female because almost all torties are female.

"Why's that?" I asked. She said a tortie's special coloring is only produced by two X chromosomes, which is what females have. Males have only one X and one Y chromosome and therefore can't inherit that coloring—unless the male cat has an extra X chromosome (XXY), like her stray baby.

"I took him to the vet," she said, "for the usual checkup. She did the bloodwork, dewormed him, clipped his nails. She said this boy's one in a thousand. That's the odds in finding a male tortie."

His name was now Nash, short for Nashville. "I could tell right away he's a rare one. He cuddles up for love more than any other cats I've had."

"That makes him a true gem," I agreed.

Lord, thank You for my unique, loving companion.

A Safe Place

This I declare about the LORD:
He alone is my refuge, my place of safety.
PSALM 91:2 NLT

Minding her own business, Barb was out watering her hostas when a drenched kitten darted out from between the plants. The feral cat made it clear she didn't like her unplanned shower. Cat lover Barb tried to approach the kitten, but she darted away from the woman who was still holding the garden hose. She didn't go far, however, and soon Barb had her literally eating out of her hand. A little fresh tuna can be enticing when food has been hard to find for a barely weaned feline.

"Smokey" is a feral cat no more. She found her safe place. Sixteen years later, the kitten who crouched in the hosta hideaway remains Barb's faithful companion.

So often the one we run from first is God—He who is in the best position to help us. A church leader in our denomination ran from God for years, in part because he was fearful of reprisals from the other terrorists with whom he had associated for most of his life before his conversion. But at the most critical juncture of his life, God delivered him miraculously to a safe place. This former terrorist knows now: God is his safe place—despite the continuing threats on his life. Like Smokey, he has stopped running, too.

If you need a safe place today, pray these words from Psalm 16:1:

_____

"Keep me safe, O God, for I have come to you for refuge."

The Crazy Cat Lady

For the grace of God has appeared that offers salvation
to all people. It teaches us to say "No" to ungodliness
and worldly passions, and to live self-controlled,
upright and godly lives in this present age.

TITUS 2:11–12 NIV

I once knew a crazy cat lady. She liked cats. They made her smile and comforted her when she was stressed. So when her cat had kittens, she kept them all.

Eventually, those cats grew up and had kittens. She tried to share them, but she couldn't find homes for them all. So she kept the ones she couldn't give away.

Those cats grew up and had kittens, and on and on, until finally her house was overtaken by cats. The problem was that although Theresa loved her pets, she didn't invest the time or money into having them neutered and spayed. The health department finally issued her a fine and forced her to get rid of all her animals.

That's how sin is if we don't take measures to stop it early. It seems fun. It offers us comfort when we're stressed. We welcome it, feed it, pet it. . .and it multiplies. Soon, we feel overrun by our sin and don't know how to get rid of it.

Whether it's gossip, gluttony, or pornography, it's easier to keep sin at bay if we take care of it when it's still small. Though it may seem inconvenient, time invested in keeping ourselves free from sin's effects is always worthwhile.

Dear Father, help me take care of sin
in my life before it gets out of control.

Climb Out of the Box

"Jerusalem, Jerusalem, you who kill the prophets and stone those sent to you, how often I have longed to gather your children together, as a hen gathers her chicks under her wings, and you were not willing."

MATTHEW 23:37 NIV

Sparkle was a beautiful calico, with brown and orange woven across her back and face, leaving her underbelly a perfect white.

When she had kittens, I marveled that the tiny newborns could fit in my child-sized hands. We moved them to a cardboard box. Soon their eyes opened and they began to crawl—and climb.

Their mother jumped in and out of the box with ease. When the kittens tried to follow, they flopped back on the soft towel. But the day came when they managed to claw their way to the top and flop onto the floor—safely, as even a kitten can manage.

I raced through the house, yelling, "The kittens got out of the box!" All too soon, they would never stay in the box. They took over the house.

In the same way, God delights in our growth, from our birth until the time we're ready to get out of the box and be light and salt in the world.

Let's be like those kittens—feed on God's Word and climb out of the box!

Dear Father, You feed and care for us and cheer
when we are ready to climb out of the box.
May we work to make You proud.

Bringing Eva Home

The LORD comforts his people and will
have compassion on his afflicted ones
ISAIAH 49:13 NKJV

In the span of one year, two of our four sons had moved into apartments with friends, another got married, and the youngest was graduating high school with plans to be a college boy. I was feeling a little lonely adjusting to it all. Caring for another little life felt very much in order. So I visited a friend with kittens and picked out a sweet, tiny gray and white fluff ball who would soon be known as Eva. She immediately curled up on my lap for the ride home, warm and sweet. I rode with the windows down on that beautiful summer night and sighed happily.

I brought her home where my oldest son, who was visiting and going through some difficulties of his own at the time, was relaxing on the couch. I brought little Eva in to meet him. She crawled up his chest, curled up on his neck, and fell asleep. He fell asleep and looked as peaceful as I'd seen him in days. God is so good to give us comfort when He knows we need it, even if it's in the little things.

Lord, thank You for seeing what we need before we do and providing even the smallest of comforts to get us through.

Visitors on My Porch

"Share your food with the hungry, and give shelter
to the homeless. Give clothes to those who need them,
and do not hide from relatives who need your help."
ISAIAH 58:7 NLT

I live out in the country and put food out for the wild cats. So many of them find their way to my front porch because they've been abandoned along the main road. The poor things have no place to go, and I don't want to see them ending up as food for the foxes who also roam this section of the valley.

It's getting cold in the evenings. I put out a lined cat box in case an animal wants to find warmth. One morning, there was a surprise in the box. I heard mewing. The most precious tan-colored kitten snuggled against the pile of old socks inside. But why was she there all alone?

I anchored my video camera in the window and set it to record. The next night, a mama cat brought four more kittens and parked them in the box. They were a family. She couldn't feed them by herself and was asking for my help. I found myself providing extra food for five plus Mama. She came and went, caring for them, too. That's a big job for one mother cat, and it was stressing her out. I put out a box for her so she could find security for herself.

Father God, help us look to the needs of
those around us, addressing both human
concerns and those of our animal friends.

No Perfect Ten

But God chose the foolish things of the world to shame the wise;
God chose the weak things of the world to shame the strong.
God chose the lowly things of this world and the despised
things. . .so that no one may boast before him.

1 CORINTHIANS 1:27–29 NIV

Nancy can't resist an injured cat. This retired teacher volunteers at
the local humane society. From there she has brought home cats
most people would never adopt. Cats with one eye, cats with three
legs—Nancy adopts and helps less-than-perfect cats live sheltered,
happy lives. At last count, she had an even half-dozen feline friends.

Jesus never turned away from "less-than-perfect" people.
"Great crowds came to him, bringing the lame, the blind, the
crippled, the mute and many others, and laid them at his feet; and
he healed them" (Matthew 15:30). We cannot heal anyone as He did,
but are we ready to minister to those who have special needs? Do
we have the same heart of tenderness as our God?

Just as Nancy has taken in and cares for unique felines, we
may cross paths with people who long for some companionship
from others willing to help them. Who knows? In doing so we may
find ourselves showing "hospitality to angels without knowing it"
(Hebrews 13:2).

Lord, give me eyes to see others as You see them.
Give me hands willing to reach out to others in need. Amen.

Mews from a Bullhorn

*Be pleasant and hold their interest when you speak
the message. Choose your words carefully and be
ready to give answers to anyone who asks questions.*
COLOSSIANS 4:6 CEV

My daughter has three kittens. August has attitude. Roger is sane and endearing. Ninja lives up to her name in every respect but her voice.

She is stealthy and devious. Crickets, grasshoppers, and mice need to beef up their cat detection skills because Ninja knows where they are and how to disable them in dramatic and intimidating ways.

Her mews, however, sound like they come from a bullhorn. If she mews, she negates the whole ninja vibe for which she was named. She can wake up the house with one jarring mew. One bad guy roaming the house would rethink his life choices at the sound of Ninja opening her mouth.

I don't really know what Ninja is trying to say, but she's committed to speaking up.

Unlike Ninja, we might know why we should speak up, but we seem to develop spiritual laryngitis. We have a life-changing message to share, but we hide in the shadows, disguise our identity, and keep our mouths shut.

Speak up. God's life-giving message may be worth a bullhorn delivery. At the very least, speak up as you walk out of the shadows.

Dear God, You want me to share Your life-changing news
with others. May I reject the shadows and show
others the light of Your love. Amen.

Bad Princess

Because the Lord disciplines those he loves,
just as a father the son he delights in.

PROVERBS 3:12 NIV

Karen, known among our friends as the Cat Lady, laughs about Princess—the meanest cat she ever met.

"I watched Princess during my friend's honeymoon for thirty days.

"When I first brought her home, Princess went ballistic. She hissed, growled, climbed the curtains and knocked down everything in her path. I gave her grace to acclimate to a strange environment.

"The second day I took her food away when she hissed and scratched. The next day when I tried to pet her, she slapped me with her claws protruded—so I tapped her head. Day four and still feisty, she did it again—I tapped her again. The next day I gave her more food by hand as she was not as resistant.

"She became less aggressive with time and received more food as a reward. If she acted out, I removed the food.

"Eventually, I stayed with her in the evenings. She started coming around to be stroked and earned more food for good conduct. Slowly, it worked. I left the door open, and she came out to socialize with my other cats. Motivated by rewards, I continued reinforcing her behavior with treats."

Karen was determined to teach Princess how to behave like a princess. She took time and effort to discipline her, much like the way God disciplines those He calls His children.

Thank You, Lord, for Your righteous
discipline that You give to Your children.

A Cat Named Dog

"Come to me, all you who are weary and burdened, and I will give you rest."
MATTHEW 11:28 NIV

Years ago, I knew a man who had a cat named "Dog." I asked him about the name, and he explained that he'd never liked cats because they didn't come when you called them. Every cat he'd ever known had been aloof and evasive, unlike dogs, whom he viewed as friendly and responsive.

One day, he noticed a cat hanging around his boat, which he kept parked in his back garage. Without thinking, he called the cat to him, and the cat came. He offered the feline some food and water, and soon the two were fast friends.

After a few weeks, it became clear that the man had a new pet. He named his cat "Dog" because he came when he was called, and the two had a long and lovely relationship.

Like that man, God calls to us. He wants to offer us spiritual food and water, shelter and comfort. Yet it's in my nature to be aloof and evasive. I want a relationship with God on my terms, not His. If I'll just come when He calls—which is every day—I'll find myself in the warm shelter of His presence. He'll clean me up, see to my needs, and give me a home. All my needs will be met in Him. . .if I'll only come.

Dear Father, forgive me for not coming when You call. I want to respond to Your love and find peace in Your presence.

Ring Nipper

If you declare with your mouth, "Jesus is Lord," and believe in your heart that God raised him from the dead, you will be saved.

ROMANS 10:9 NIV

When I was traveling through Nebraska, I spent the night in my sister's guest room. Besides having a comfy bed, it came equipped with two large cats, Hank and Pistol. Pistol didn't pay me much attention, but Hank loved to have his short golden fur stroked. He liked it so much that he would nip my wedding ring to get me to pet him some more.

I thought it was very clever that he'd get my attention this way. He made sure I knew what he wanted, but by nipping my ring instead of my finger, he didn't hurt me. I told my nephew, the cat's owner, this, and he was surprised. He had never seen his cat do that before.

Sometimes you think you know someone, but then they surprise you. We can read the Bible over and over, but God always has a surprise or two for His kids. He has clever ways to get our attention, too. People often wonder why God allows bad things in our lives. Sometimes it's to get our attention, but ultimately these things won't hurt us. Even if we die, we are promised eternal life when we put our faith and trust in Jesus.

Thank You, Lord of the Universe, that You desire my attention.
I set all things aside right now and simply adore You.
I am truly grateful for Your love.

Saved

But you are God's chosen and special people. You are a group of royal priests and a holy nation. God has brought you out of darkness into his marvelous light. Now you must tell all the wonderful things that he has done.

1 PETER 2:9 CEV

"Mama Cat," a feral stray that adopted Paula and Red, hid her kittens each year in the strangest places on their property. One fall afternoon, Paula listened intently to the meows of newborn kittens up a tree not far from the back porch. Paula hadn't seen "Mama Cat" that morning. That evening, the kittens became stranded during a storm that was expected to turn violent.

Paula persuaded Red to go out into the rain and save them. She stood with an umbrella and held a flashlight until they were all placed safely into a laundry basket full of towels. Inside the house, she checked each one to make sure they were okay.

There was still no sign of "Mama Cat" the next morning, so Red went to the feed store for bottles and kitten formula. Months later, they sat on the porch, waiting for a young family to arrive to adopt the last little kitten. "You saved those kittens," Red said. "It makes me think about how Jesus saved me. On a dark night when all seemed lost, He reached in and saved me."

Jesus, thank You for saving me. When I thought I was alone and lost, You reached down and promised to always be with me.

143

The Case of the Missing Cat

" 'For this son of mine was dead and is alive again;
he was lost and is found.' So they began to celebrate."
LUKE 15:24 NIV

Mike, my tiger Manx cat, was the son of my first pet, Sparkle. We did everything together, even when he tried to stop me from playing clarinet by jumping in my lap and howling.

One day, Mike decided to follow me to high school. He kept company with me as I walked down the steep hill to downtown Augusta, Maine. With each block, I begged him to go home. What would happen when I arrived at school? He couldn't find his way home.

Something even worse happened: halfway across the Kennebec River, where I would climb another hill to reach my high school, he left me. Sure enough, when I got home hours later, he wasn't there. I resigned myself to the loss of my kitty.

Three days later, he showed up at the doorstep as if he had only been gone for a couple of hours.

How my family rejoiced that night, like the banquet the father in the parable threw for his prodigal son.

We may follow God in the same way Mike followed me that day—tag along faithfully for a while and then go astray. When we admit our sin, He welcomes us home with rejoicing.

Come on home.

Lord, we confess that we run away from You.
We thank You that You welcome us back, ready to forgive.

Finding the Way

You will show me the way of life, granting me the joy of your
presence and the pleasures of living with you forever.
PSALM 16:11 NLT

Children love baby animals. Even teenage boys who like to act
macho turn tender around tiny kittens. They also invent things to
do that only guys would think of and hate to admit that they really
like playing with cute little fluff balls.

Our cat gave us a litter of five, and while the kittens were too
small to play with, our children were content to watch Lucy tenderly
care for her babies. But they grew fast, so before long the boys were
challenged to create an interesting game.

They started with a couple cardboard boxes and duct tape.
They taped the boxes together and cut a door between. Then they
added extra boxes, more doors, some steps, boxes within boxes, and
a lot of imagination to create a complicated maze. Add kittens and
let the games begin.

Our boys tried to confuse the baby cats by putting them in
different corners. When they found their way around, the kids
moved walls to complicate things, but the kittens grew adept at
finding how one path led to one another. They romped in their
playground till exhaustion and hunger took over. But after naps and
a meal, they were eager to resume their play.

Heavenly Father, thank You for leading us through the
maze of life. You always show us the way of love and joy.

Always Hope

"Do not look at his appearance or at his physical stature, because I have refused him. For the LORD does not see as man sees; for man looks at the outward appearance, but the LORD looks at the heart."

1 SAMUEL 16:7 NKJV

Mangy, tiny, and nearly lifeless, the calico, Kolat, made almost no noise. My son, Mitch, found her alongside the building outside the wrestling room after practice on a cold, snowy night and brought her home wrapped in a sweatshirt. "She's still alive, Mom. Do you think she'll make it?" We didn't know, but we would try. We warmed her up, cleaned her eyes, and heated some milk for her. She accepted all of these things and gave us hope that she would pull through. We made her a shelter—our standard box on its side with a towel for a bedding and a warmer underneath. She had everything a struggling kitten could need under the circumstances, but she didn't make it.

Every time I think of my son's heart to save this little life, I am touched. He didn't think about how bad things looked but rather looked at the hope for healing and life.

Lord, thank You for seeing the heart of things, the potential for healing and wholeness in me. You are so good to me.

Who Let the Cats Out?

Devote yourselves to prayer,
being watchful and thankful.
COLOSSIANS 4:2 NIV

Jason and Cathy like to sit outdoors on their back patio and relax.
Their two cats are indoor cats and must stay inside. Jax and Helio
don't like that. The "boys" think they're missing out on the fun when
they see Mom and Dad lounging in the fresh air without them.
Unfair, when frisky felines are left pacing on the windowsill!

The couple decided to install a chain link fence around the
backyard to provide a safe haven for their pets. The project was
more complicated than they had anticipated. City building codes
required them to schedule and pay for a visit from a code inspector.
The expense of installation was greater than anticipated, but
eventually the fence went up with a cat guard all around the top.
The netting was higher than the two cats could jump.

So far, so good. The couple let the cats outside when someone
was out there to watch them. But one day, Cathy got a call. "That
white cat of yours is walking up our driveway." She looked out back
and saw her husband napping. The gate stood open. Did the cats
jump at the latch? Did a neighbor child open the gate? No one
knows.

The couple retrieved their pets safely and installed a lock on
the gate. Live and learn.

Help us, Father in heaven, to be ever watchful
of all the creatures You place in our care.

Impressionable

"Whoever welcomes one of these little children in my name welcomes me."

MARK 9:37 NIV

We always had pets when I was growing up. When *The Lady and The Tramp* came out, I was shocked (and maybe a bit traumatized) by the Siamese cats in the movie. The talk around the block afterward was "Cats suck the air out of babies because they smell milk." A line in the "Siamese Cat Song" hints at the likelihood of such—or it did back then to a bunch of elementary children. All of us made sure no cats got into the same room as any of our sleeping infant siblings. Those cats, that song, and our own rumor mill had us all scared spitless (as people used to say) of cats getting into our families' baby cribs.

Children are impressionable, aren't they? We remember things from our childhood that, for good or bad, we cannot forget. Whether they are song lyrics or unkind words, those things that misled or hurt us may be the hardest to shake.

Little wonder the Lord instructs us to be careful in our words and our treatment of children. He continues on in Mark 9, saying, "If anyone causes one of these little ones—those who believe in me—to stumble, it would be better for them if a large millstone were hung around their neck and they were thrown into the sea" (Mark 9:42).

Lord, give me the sensitivity
to childrenb. Amen.

Zelda the Kangaroo

"Be glad; rejoice forever in my creation!"
ISAIAH 65:18 NLT

It was one of those moments that I needed someone else to witness, or no one would have believed me.

My son Trevor and I walked out in the backyard as our tiny cat, Zelda, ran over to greet us. She was so happy to see us that she hopped about five times on her hind legs, leaping in fast-forward. Covering a lot of ground with a few hind footsteps, she looked much more like a kangaroo than a cat. Frozen in our tracks, Trevor and I looked at one another in utter shock. "No one will believe us," Trevor said. We retold the story several times that evening and laughed all over again.

The quirks and affections of this cat just keep coming. What a joy it is to see the uniqueness and complexity of God's creation.

Father God, thank You for showing me a bit of Yourself in. . . yes, my cat. Help me to see You today in multiple ways in the midst of the many distractions and duties of life.

Talia the Sia-Tai Cat

Everyone who is left alive in
Jerusalem will be called special.
ISAIAH 4:3 CEV

Talia was the most unusual cat I had ever seen. Her blue eyes and soft seal point ears and tail suggested that she was a Siamese cat, but her beige fur lay beneath tiger markings. I assumed she had a Siamese parent and a tiger parent, and so I called her a Sia-Tai mix.

Talia also had the high-pitched yowl of the Siamese breed and was just as intelligent. Owning a Siamese cat (or did she own me?) was a dream come true.

Several years later, someone let me in on a secret. Talia wasn't a Siamese/tiger mix; she was a rare breed known as a lynx point Siamese.

Talia hadn't changed—but she had been reclassified. Instead of an ordinary American shorthair cat, she was a rare breed.

We may feel like that, too—an ordinary person of no special importance. The people left in Jerusalem after the deportation felt that way—one translation describes them as "discards" and "rejects."

God stepped in. They weren't discards anymore. They were holy, special—precious.

Once, we were dead, nobodies in the depths of sin. Then God stepped in and brought us back to life. In His sight, we are holy, His most precious belongings.

Abba Father, thank You for choosing me
and making me Your precious child. May my
behavior declare Your presence in my life.

The Flipper

Dear friends, since God so loved us,
we also ought to love one another.

1 JOHN 4:11 NIV

Cats have their ways of getting attention: bunting (rubbing and head bumping), sitting on your laptop, joining you in the bathroom where you're a captive audience, kneading (rhythmically pushing their paws on soft surfaces that carry your scent), and flipping (throwing themselves at your feet and rolling back and forth).

My sister's cat, Bensley, is a flipper. She flips and flops on my sister's lap. She likes to be held like a baby and will purr and go to sleep in her arms. Bensley also likes to lie upside down on my sister's lap with her head to the floor, looking like an awkward gymnast. All of these attention-getting tactics are also ways of expressing her affection.

When they feel they are not getting enough attention, cats get persistent to the point of being a nuisance, obnoxious, or even avoiding you. Humans can be the same with God, to the point of throwing fits or giving God the cold shoulder. How do we get God's attention? Do we just want something, or do we want to show our affection? Worship is a key component to a Christian's life. Instead of bringing Him our wish lists, let's curl up on His lap, like Bensley, and get comfortable. However, the best way to show our love for God is to love others.

God, help me express my love for You by actively worshipping You and loving others.

Can You Take My Cat?

*He could also speak about animals, birds, small creatures,
and fish. And kings from every nation sent their
ambassadors to listen to the wisdom of Solomon.*

1 KINGS 4:33–34 NLT

Sometimes I wish I could call upon the wisdom of Solomon,
especially when a friend or acquaintance asks me, "You have cats.
My mom's going into a nursing home. My son's allergic to cats.
Would you be willing to take Sheba for us?"

Goodness. I love animals as much as anyone and want to see
all pets in happy homes. I know the person who asks a favor like
this is going through a tough time transitioning someone to a
nursing home and trying to find a forever home for a pet. But it's not
fair to me, my family, or my own cats. We have constraints on our
time. My cats may not accept the new arrival. A newcomer will bring
maintenance and veterinarian fees. When pets get older, there are
end-of-life issues.

In cases like this, I promise to call the pet ministry at my
church. They're a great group, and many churches have developed a
similar help ministry for owners who can no longer care for or feed
their pets. They collect donations to buy animal food for owners
who are going through financial problems. They have volunteers
who have signed up on a waiting list to take pets into their homes.
It's a great way to love the family of God by caring for the furry
members of their families.

Lord, help us be sensitive to even the
smallest of needs of fellow pet owners.

Wild Thing

"The Lord disciplines the one he loves."
HEBREWS 12:6 NIV

Splash had her way of doing things. She was birthed in the wild. When she found herself a family cat, she still insisted on doing things her way. She refused to use a litter box and instead would go to the door and let Nancy know she needed to go out. When she gave birth to her litter of kittens, she determined her brood would be well suited for work outside, just as she was. She brought a live mouse into the house to train them in proper mousing technique. They learned quickly and well.

Nancy says that in spite of her independence, Splash was the best cat they ever had. And there must be something to that outdoor living: she lived twenty years.

Properly disciplined and lovingly reared, strong-willed children often grow up to be good leaders. A friend of ours tells us that he, as a missionary himself, works with many other strong-willed missionaries. "We're type A personalities," he says, laughing. "The Lord has wired us for difficult service in difficult places."

"Direct your children onto the right path, and when they are older, they will not leave it," the Lord commands parents of all children (Proverbs 22:6 NLT). He's not asking us to do anything He doesn't do with His own. The rest of the above verse from Hebrews reads, "and he chastens everyone he accepts as his son."

Thank you, Lord, for Your loving discipline.

Cleo

Understanding is a wellspring of life unto him that hath it.
PROVERBS 16:22 KJV

Mom's cat, Cleo, is a lot of work. She sprayed in the house when Mom brought her home, and she clawed and peed on the furniture. The house reeked. Mom complained so much that I encouraged her to return Cleo to the SPCA.

"Aww, I can't do that," she would mumble whenever the suggestion surfaced.

Mom figured out a way to keep Cleo. She watches her closely to intervene before she wets the blue recliner. She puts Cleo out in the garage to sleep so she can't pee in her room at night.

Meat treats in a special jar indicate Cleo's bedtime. Mom rattles the jar lid and Cleo runs to the kitchen, meowing and shuddering her tail.

"Sometimes I tease her with only one tablespoon of meat. She scowls at me and yells as if saying, 'Give me my meat!' " Mom laughs.

"Then we head to the garage. Cleo *always* stops right in front of me and slowly stretches before she skitters out the door. She's a funny cat!"

Mom's compassion kept her from giving up on Cleo. She made adjustments to live with her and enjoys her antics. The house doesn't smell anymore.

It may take time to accept people with seemingly intolerable habits. But if we find the humor in the differences and have the empathy to stick it out, we may learn to love them.

Grant me humor and patience, Lord, to find answers
to challenging people and situations in my life.

Family Comfort

*Let us consider how we may spur one another on toward love
and good deeds, not giving up meeting together, as some
are in the habit of doing, but encouraging one another.*
HEBREWS 10:24–25 NIV

Nipper perched on anything that got him away from the family
dogs. He refused to be bothered by their enthusiasm.

Nipper wasn't always the equivalent of a feline couch potato.
Once he was young and insisted on chasing the heels of the five
children in the home. Nipping at their feet was how he got his
name. He was no longer in nip-and-run condition.

When I first met my wife, this was her family's cat. Nipper
looked to my wife for protection and would rest against her head at
the top of the bed each night.

This had been his forever home, and he was loyal. Even when
he wasn't very active, there was no doubt he was comfortable,
knowing he was with family.

Christians have family, too. When we gather, we may have the
enthusiasm of a kitten or the limited movement of one who simply
observes after many years, but in a forever family, *everyone* is
needed.

Dear God, You want me to get along with those
You call family. Help me understand that Your love
for me is extended to everyone I meet. And even
when it's hard to love everyone, help me remember
how much it cost Your Son to show love to me.
Help me love those who share my journey. Amen.

Tom-Kitty

I know what it is to be in need, and I know what it is to have plenty. I have learned the secret of being content in any and every situation, whether well fed or hungry, whether living in plenty or in want.

PHILIPPIANS 4:12 NIV

Tom-Kitty didn't know his place. He was an outside cat. . .except he didn't want to be an outside cat. Every time the door opened, he squeezed through the opening and found a hiding place in the house. Once he hid behind the refrigerator, and my husband had to move the huge appliance just to get Tom-Kitty out.

Now Tom-Kitty had a pretty good life outdoors. He had a nice warm garage with a bed, plenty of food, and a space heater in the winter. He had a freshwater pond he could drink from and lots of space to roam. But he just wouldn't be content with his lot in life. Because of that, he caused himself and everyone else a lot of unneeded stress.

Much of the stress in our lives is brought about because we refuse to be content. We fail to give thanks for the blessings we already have. Instead, we long for things someone else has, and we spend our time trying to figure out how to get something different.

If we'll just learn to be content in whatever situation God places us, we'll soon realize that the key to harnessing the joy and peace we really want lies in appreciating what we already have.

Dear Father, thank You for my blessings.
Help me to be content.

Roadkill Redemption

"'I will rescue you from their bondage, and I will redeem you with an outstretched arm and with great judgments.'"
EXODUS 6:6 NKJV

Out for a jog one weekend on a country road, I saw what looked like a small dead animal along the side of the road. As it was directly in my path, I planned to sidestep around it. As I approached, it jumped up! Nearly twisting my ankle from the jolt of surprise, I jumped back to collect myself. A striped, brown little cat greeted me, rubbing her chin on my leg before curling up to snuggle at my ankles. Elated to see me, this cat would not leave my side. I knew that if I left her she would likely be roadkill. So I called my youngest son, Dexter, who had run the same route just half an hour earlier. I planned to ask him to come pick up the cat in the car, but before I said anything he asked, "Are you calling about that cat along the side of the road?" My family knows me.

He came and picked up the cat. We named her Zelda since she was a road warrior and all. Each time I fed her or cared for her, she was grateful. I couldn't help but think about how God rescued me in similar but far greater ways.

Lord, thank You for redeeming me from my
own certain demise. I am eternally grateful
for Your love and care for me.

Cat Rescuers

In your righteousness, rescue me and deliver me;
turn your ear to me and save me.

PSALM 71:2 NIV

In the movies, the friendly fireman will rescue a cat that gets stuck in a tree.

In real life, the dispatcher laughed when my ginger cat, Sally, climbed to the top of a tall oak tree in our front yard. "Just wait. She'll find her way down."

Except—she didn't. She stayed in the tree one day, howling. Two days—the neighbors complained. Three days—they demanded a resolution. We had to find a solution.

Without a ladder, we chose the only available option. I climbed through the window of my daughter's bedroom onto the roof. Slowly, carefully, I inched down the incline.

I don't remember the rest. Did she jump to me? Did I latch on to her? Did I lasso her with a towel? Whatever I did, Sally returned to the safety of the house, the security of constant food (from a self-feeder bowl), and all the water she needed.

Like the cat in the tree, we all have times we know we are in trouble. We may turn to professionals for help, but they say it's our responsibility. We wait. Other people notice. Finally we take the risk, climb out on the roof—and reach out and help.

God is ready to grab our hand and help us inside.

God our Rescuer, thank You for answering our calls for help.

Identity Theft

*Once you were like sheep who wandered away. But now you
have turned to your Shepherd, the Guardian of your souls.*

1 PETER 2:25 NLT

Betty's black cat, Freddy, wasn't content to stay inside. He'd doze
near a door, but if the door opened even a crack, he made a dash
for freedom. Most times Freddy's mistress could intercept him, but
occasionally he escaped. And if you've ever tried to catch a cat that
doesn't want to be caught, you know what a challenge it was to
retrieve him.

Freddy usually came home before nighttime, sometimes a
little bedraggled, content to stay inside—until the next opportunity.
But one evening he stayed out, and finding a black cat after dark is
almost impossible.

The next morning, there he was, sunning himself on Betty's
front stoop. She scooped him up, called him a naughty cat, and told
him how happy she was to see him. Then she served him breakfast.
He felt lighter, like he'd lost weight overnight, and he wolfed down
his food.

After eating, Freddy stretched out on his back, and Betty had a
shocking realization. This was definitely not Freddy.

Betty ran to the door, searching for the real Freddy. And at that
moment, another black cat bounded across the lawn toward the house.
The cats looked almost identical, but there was only one Freddy.

Dear Lord, help me never to run from You. I want
to be content and stay near You, trusting You to be my
guardian. Thank You that You never mistake Your children!
As our Good Shepherd, You are always watching over us.

My Best Friend, Gabby O' Goober

*Let us continue to love one another, for love comes from God.
Anyone who loves is a child of God and knows God.
But anyone who does not love does not know God, for God is love.*

1 JOHN 4:7–8 NLT

Gabby, a white male cat, lived on the front porch of my parents' house. He made his living as a wonderful mouser on their seven-acre property. As an older cat, he lived life on his own terms. Sometimes he avoided all human contact, other times he insisted you scratch his neck or pet his back.

My son, Bryce, who was three at the time, loved this temperamental old cat. He would run onto the porch looking for Gabby as soon as we arrived at my parents' house after the five-hour drive. Once he found the cat, often sleeping in the sun on the front porch, he'd call to him saying, "Gabby O' Goober, you're my best friend."

It didn't matter what that cat did or didn't do, Bryce's love for this cat was unconditional. The cat would get up and leave, completely ignoring Bryce. He might roll over and let Bryce pet him. It just depended on what kind of mood the usually grouchy cat was in.

One time, Bryce reached out to stroke his head and the cat nipped him. The look on Bryce's face said it all. He was heartbroken that his best friend would do that! I expected him to become angry at the cat. Instead, he climbed up into the porch swing next to my mom and said, "He's kinda grouchy, but Gabby O' Goober is still my best friend!"

---

*Heavenly Father, thank You for Your unconditional love.
Show me how to love others unconditionally,
even when they disappoint or hurt me.*

When Everything Is New

I lay down and slept, yet I woke up in safety,
for the LORD was watching over me.
PSALM 3:5 NLT

"Baby sweets, eat your yum yums," I tell my new kitty. Just brought her home three days ago. I have her eating a bit of baby food. Her favorite is chicken Beech-Nut. I put a dab on my finger and let her sniff. Then I wiggle my finger near the opening of her mouth. When she's receptive, I scoop it in. She sucks on it, and it goes down the hatch. She thinks this is play and tries to bite me.

No big deal. She'll get the hang of eating on her own soon. I'm also patient in teaching her to use the litter box. She's confined to my small living room area so she'll always be near the box. She's too young to understand why I set her up down there. Every time she lets loose somewhere else, it's a mess to clean up.

Again, no big deal. She's my little love. We'll grow in this thing together. She's my angel sent from above so I send a prayer upward, *Keep my baby safe.* Heaven knows, I'm doing my part.

Sometimes we forget what it's like to be a baby and all alone in the world. May God help me always to remember as she grows that I'm her guide and caregiver.

Thank You, Lord, for giving us peace of mind that we can then pass on to others, including our beloved pets.

Welcomed In

Because of his great love for us, God, who is rich in mercy,
made us alive with Christ even when we were dead in
transgressions—it is by grace you have been saved.
EPHESIANS 2:4–5 NIV

All her life Margie has had dogs. When a feral cat showed up at her house, she kept waiting for—and encouraging—her cat-loving neighbors to take in the stray. When no one did, Margie had a pet door entrance put into her attached garage so the black and white tuxedo cat could come in out of the weather.

Margie still had her dogs, but she decided they could make room for Fred, too. It wasn't long before Fred Astaire (the cat, not the late dancer) had the run of the house. Whenever the dogs come back from any outing, they give Fred a kiss of greeting.

"We're back! Let's all snuggle in for Animal Planet."

God doesn't welcome us to Himself because of our appearance or demeanor. He knows us for who we are, warts and all. We can only approach Him humbly, recognizing our need for His forgiveness and being cleansed from sin. One of the Bible's greatest statements of the magnitude of God's grace follows a man's simple plea: " 'God, have mercy on me, a sinner.' This man. . ." Jesus declared, "went home justified before God" (Luke 18:13–14). He was not only forgiven, but God declared him righteous!

Have you done as the man in Jesus' parable did? God stands ready to welcome you in.

Father God, forgive me for my sin against You.

Comforter

This is my comfort in my affliction,
that your promise gives me life.
PSALM 119:50 ESV

I grew up with dogs. I'd never been around cats at all, so I considered myself a dog person until I was in college. Then one weekend, I visited a friend. I was having one of those down-in-the-dumps, pity-party kinds of moments: my boyfriend and I weren't getting along, I'd failed a test, and on top of it all, I hated my new haircut.

Late that night, I lay in the guest room bed of my friend's home and cried. That's when I felt a warm presence press against my back. It was my friend's cat, Dee-Dee.

Now, Dee-Dee had never given me the time of day before. She ignored me and hid when I came near. But somehow she must have sensed I needed a friend, and she reached out to me. At least, that's how I saw her actions that night.

I rolled over and scrunched my hands in her fur, and she purred. And somehow, things didn't seem quite so bad.

Sometimes it feels like God hides from us. Sometimes it seems like He doesn't have time for our problems or we're not important to Him. But He's there. He knows. And when we finally allow ourselves to be still and quiet, we'll feel Him near us, reminding us we're loved and we're not alone.

Dear Father, thank You for comforting me
when I need comfort. Remind me of Your
presence when it feels like You're hiding.

The Plan Came Together

We know that God causes everything to work together for the good of those who love God and are called according to his purpose for them.
ROMANS 8:28 NLT

I wanted the best for Annie, but I wasn't sure I was the right owner for this gray feline.

Scott was Annie's owner. We had worked together, and he was leaving town to take on a new job. Annie couldn't come with him, and he needed a new home for his friend.

I already had a dog and wasn't sure it would work out, but Scott had the persistent whine of a two-year-old at nap time.

Finally, taking my hearing and sanity into account, I took Annie home and Scott left town. The next morning Annie escaped, and I thought she was gone for good—and she was.

A month later, I noticed the kids next door hovering over something and laughing. In the middle of their huddle sat the prodigal Annie. She had left to pick her own family. She chose well.

It wasn't how I planned it, but Annie was just perfect for those two kids and their parents. In the end, Annie got the best, and I was more than okay with that.

Dear God, You want me to know that even when things
don't work out like I plan—Your plan will still work out.
You know where You're going. Help me trust
You during each turn in the journey. Amen.

Crazy Love

Above all, love each other deeply,
because love covers over a multitude of sins.
1 PETER 4:8 NIV

"I have two cats that fight all day," Elaine explained.

"They scratch at each other when I try to snuggle with them on my bed. They chase each other off the couch during the day and drive each other crazy, swatting when one gets too close to the other.

"Then, every night they retire to the laundry room together, and suddenly—they're buds! They knock their heads together in love, lick each other's ears, and sleep in the same bed.

"They fuss all day, but at night when it's time to sleep, they are lovey and affectionate."

Even as Elaine is mystified by her cats' behavior, human relationships can be perplexing, too.

Do you have a sibling, spouse, or child whom you love very much, but it seems like you two can argue about everything? If you want to go right, they pick left. If you try to please them, they are not impressed. And just maybe they feel like they can't please you either! Mind boggling, isn't it?

Some very special relationships that God has given us may not work smoothly. Like sandpaper, these refining relationships rub out our rough edges. We may not fully understand what's behind the irritations, but we can overlook them and reassure each other often of our love.

Lord, deepen our love to overlook the irritants
and create special moments to share and
care with those we love so much.

Vanna White

I praise you because I am fearfully and wonderfully made;
your works are wonderful, I know that full well.
PSALM 139:14 NIV

Vanna was originally brought into our home to run off some of the rodents in our yard. At least, that was our intention. She had other ideas.

She grew into a beautiful silky white diva. She didn't like to go outdoors; she preferred her comfy bed near the dryer, or better yet, a corner of the living room couch. She liked to be spoiled and pampered, and she was very good at making her demands known.

We wanted a mouser. A predator. A huntress.

We got a fluffy pink-and-sparkles girly girl.

And we loved her to distraction.

Sometimes we don't live up to other people's expectations of us. They want us to be a certain way, but that's just not who we are. But God, who created us exactly as He wanted us, loves us to distraction. We were each made with unique gifts and a unique purpose—even if that purpose is just to delight our Father.

When we try to live up to unrealistic expectations, we often fail. But when we embrace the person God created us to be and live to please Him alone by serving Him and loving others, we will find contentment.

Dear Father, thank You for making me unique. Help me
to be satisfied with Your purpose for me. I want
to honor You with my choices and actions.

Legacy

But with eager hope, the creation looks forward to the day when it will join God's children in glorious freedom from death and decay.

ROMANS 8:20–21 NLT

Years ago, our beloved brown-black striped family cat, Ed, named after one of the noisy hyenas in *The Lion King*, moved to California. A fierce hunter on our Ohio farm, over the years he had managed to catch rabbits while also being a gentle friend who knew when you needed a little comforting. If no one needed comforting, he was fine by himself, thank you.

When he was eleven years old and slowing down, we decided to get a kitten, hoping to bring back a bit of youth in him. It worked, after the two-day batting and hissing initiation.

Ed started training little Bruce, who looked strikingly like him. While showing him who was boss, he helped him hone great wrestling and hunting skills. Inside the house, he showed him how to pull french door ajar and slide the screen open. Watching this progress was fascinating. The day came, though, when Bruce grew so strong and able that he knocked his elder Ed onto his back. A stunning moment—and a humbled Ed walked away as if to say his work was done. That following year, he became ill and a walk westward was the last we saw of him. We are quite sure that he moved to California.

God, thank You for the powerful lessons of legacy that You give us through Your creation.

Talia the Talker

Let the redeemed of the LORD tell their story—
those he redeemed from the hand of the foe.

PSALM 107:2 NIV

The last few years I lived at home, my poor kitty, Talia, spent a lot of time alone. Each of my multiple hospital visits lasted at least a week. Friends stopped by to check on my cat, but she was alone most of the time.

The night I returned home, Talia jumped on the bed and talked to me all afternoon, all evening, and even when I was trying to sleep. It sounded like a minute-by-minute accounting of everything that had happened during my absence.

After a few days, she forgave me. She'd curl up by my side, let me pet her, and purr. But she didn't forget. The next time I had to leave, she climbed into my suitcase as soon as I opened it. If I was going somewhere, she was going with me.

I've done the same thing a time or two with God. I keep written prayer journals, and I'm ashamed of the blank pages. If I could dial into heaven's band on the radio, I might hear the same kind of pleading, anger, and confusion that Talia poured into my ears the night I came home.

The next time I go on vacation, I'll be sure to pack God along with my clothes.

Omnipresent God, forgive me for the times I forget to acknowledge Your presence. Make my heart Your home.

Shelter from the Storm

"I would hurry to my place of shelter,
far from the tempest and storm."

PSALM 55:8 NIV

I offered to share half my table at the winter craft show with my friend, Ginny. She makes kitty condos for a reasonable price and sells them to fund community education projects. Her passion is educating the public about the proper care of pets during inclement weather. She also volunteers at a rescue shelter. Her rescue boxes were a good fit with the knitted pet sweaters and catnip treats I sold on my half of our table.

We both sold items that caused visitors to stop and chat. That's half the fun of sitting for six hours in a crowded auditorium. Attendees stared at Ginny's boxes wrapped with duct tape and stuffed with shredded newspaper and asked, "What's that?"

"It's a cat rescue box," she explained. "I put these on my patio in cold weather so cats without a home can find shelter." She wraps duct tape around all the surfaces of a small Styrofoam box with a lid, then cuts a six-inch flap for an entrance. She stuffs it with insulation like hardwood shavings or straw.

"Place it on a flat Styrofoam sheet under an overhang to keep snow and rain off," she advised. "Anchor it with bricks so it doesn't blow away. Put a plastic water dish and food dish outside the box. You may save a cat's life."

Lord, may we remember animal rescue
shelters who always welcome contributions
for upkeep and community education.

Snuggling In

"He [God] is not far from any one of us.
For in him we live and move and exist."

ACTS 17:27–28 NLT

Gizmo has no particular fondness for Melissa's children, Vincent and LilyAnn. Though quite willing to share the house and yard with them, Gizmo prefers that they keep to themselves and leave him alone.

All that changes when one of the children is sick—Gizmo undergoes a transformation! Melissa may be the one to administer medicine and loving care to her ailing child, but Gizmo does what cats do best. Snuggling up with whoever is sick, he takes his place as a purring sentinel. If Vincent or LilyAnn is "down," Gizmo curls up with his sick young master or mistress and stays there until the sick child is better. Then he's back to being his old standoffish self.

For many of us, our most frightening times come with illness. We wonder if the Lord listens to our pleas when physical suffering overwhelms us. Does He hear our cries for relief?

The Bible tells us we can rest assured that the one who gives a mom the tenderness needed for an ailing child—or a cat who instinctively comforts that same child—remains close at hand, too. As the Bible reminds us, God "cares about you" (1 Peter 5:7).

Heavenly Father, when those close to me
are suffering, give me a willing heart and
hands ready to help. In Christ's name, amen.

Family Cat

And this is my prayer: that your love may abound
more and more in knowledge and depth of insight.
PHILIPPIANS 1:9 NIV

Karen regularly prays for her cats, especially her affectionate one, Sissy.

"My husband and boys used to take our Pomeranian, Puma, and black Lab, Sugar, for daily walks. One evening, our youngest son mentioned to me, 'You know, Sissy is following us around the block when we walk the dogs.'

"I didn't believe it, so I spied on them when they left the next day. Sure enough, Sissy darted from the garage and tagged behind them until their return home.

"After that, I bought a cat harness. When the boys leashed the dogs, I leashed Sissy. She didn't fight the harness. It's like she was saying, 'I get to go now, too!'

"She and Puma vied for the lead. Puma would scamper a nose ahead, then Sissy would rush a whisker ahead. It was a footrace—now Puma in the lead—now Sissy." Karen laughed.

"Sissy didn't know walks were for dogs. She especially enjoyed her family time on a leash—even if she was a cat."

Karen was open to Sissy's unique personality because she prayed.

Have we limited the opportunities we can give someone because of our own preconceived ideas? Maybe if we pray and remain open to God's leading, we will be pleasantly surprised and they will be truly blessed.

Lord, please grant me Your awareness of those around me,
that I may bless them as You have blessed me.

The Master

*Thou art worthy, O Lord, to receive glory and honour
and power: for thou hast created all things,
and for thy pleasure they are and were created.*

REVELATION 4:11 KJV

Barney likes his meals served on top of the dryer. Maybe it's warm up there; maybe he likes the view. But the minute anyone tries to give him his food and water on the floor, or any place other than the top of the dryer, Barney loses all his cuddly-cat cuteness and turns into Scar from *The Lion King*.

For some reason, Barney forgets who the master is. He thinks he has the right to call the shots. And although I laugh at Barney's superior attitude, I've realized something about myself. I've been guilty of treating God the same way. I'll act all sweet and worshipful, giving Him my love and praise. . .as long as things are exactly the way I want them. But the minute my life becomes unsettled and difficult, the minute things don't go my way, I can get a bigger-than-Texas attitude.

I forget, sometimes, who the Master is, too. He's not here to serve me. Oh, He cares for me and does all kinds of things to show His love. But when it comes down to it, He's not obligated to feed me my dinner on the dryer or give me a nice car or a fancy house. He's not obligated to bless me in any way. When I remember that, the blessings become even more special, because they remind me just how much He loves me.

Dear Father, forgive me for expecting
You to serve me. I want to serve You.

Doorstep Orphan

For I assisted. . .the orphans who required help.

JOB 29:12 NLT

A scrawny patchwork of orange, black, and white fur squatted on my doormat when I came home from work. My tuxedo cat, Sammy, watched her from inside the window.

The calico scurried away when I approached. Good. I couldn't afford another mouth to feed.

She returned the next day.

I picked her up. A closer look broke my heart. Her dull eyes conveyed hopelessness. Fleas crawled over her wasted body.

My veterinarian agreed to see her that evening. The vet tech bathed her before the doctor examined her.

"She's starving and probably won't survive the month. . .without your help."

Oh, rip my heart right out of my chest. I patted her now clean and fluffy head.

He added, "Sammy could use a companion."

How could I adopt her? She nuzzled my hand and purred. How could I not?

"I can't afford another pet."

"We'll work out a payment plan."

"I'll keep her until I find a suitable home."

"Right." A smirk followed his dubious expression. "Bring her back in a month."

We headed for home, loaded with vitamins and special food.

Four weeks later, the doctor beamed. "She's ready for that suitable home."

"We found one," I said with a wink. "Mine. Her name is Mandi."

Gracious Lord, You brought this precious orphan
into my life. Thank You for providing the means
to care for her and for fifteen years of joy.

The Lost Is Found

*"Or what woman, having ten silver coins, if she loses one coin,
does not light a lamp, sweep the house, and search carefully
until she finds it? And when she has found it, she calls her
friends and neighbors together, saying, 'Rejoice with me,
for I have found the piece which I lost!'"*

LUKE 15:8–9 NKJV

When Janice rented her first apartment, her childhood friend, a
cat called Fidge, came with her. Fidge wasn't too certain about
the new place. It certainly didn't feel like home. Just weeks after
the move, Fidge escaped through the front door one evening and
disappeared. Frantic, Janice alerted everyone she knew to be on
the lookout for Fidge.

Weeks passed, and Janice imagined Fidge had set out to find
her way back to her old house. She knew Fidge would have to trek
across the lake over a two-lane bridge that led into town in order to
make it back to her parents' house. She asked the Lord to help Fidge
find her way safely home.

Deep into the third week, Janice's father called. Fidge showed
up on the front porch of Janice's parents' home. Janice raced to see
her. Thankful to have found her furry friend, Janice decided to let
her stay with her parents.

Lord, thank You for caring about what's important
to me. Thank You for protecting and caring
for my safety and all of those I love!

Along for the Ride

" 'I carried you on eagles' wings and brought you to myself.' "
EXODUS 19:4 NIV

Why Frank named his cat after a brand of toilet paper I do not know. It's not part of this devotional thought anyway, so just come along for the ride.

While Frank cuts the grass, Charmin goes along for a ride of his own by sitting on Frank's shoulder. Around the yard they go; Charmin never falls off. He looks like a parrot perched there, but a parrot he's not. When this part-Siamese cat is not riding shotgun with his master, Charmin can be found hanging out in the bird feeder. And no, he's not there for the birdseed.

On some days, nothing goes well or right for us. We go round and round, but it's not a fun ride. Daily stresses start to define our lives. The Word of God assures us of God's constant care. God tells us that He is present to carry His own. "There you saw how the LORD your God carried you, as a father carries his son" (Deuteronomy 1:31). "Even to your old age and gray hairs I am he, I am he who will sustain you. I have made you and I will carry you" (Isaiah 46:4). I'm ready for that kind of ride!

Father, when I feel like something the cat dragged in,
remind me that You still carry me, and someday
You will bring me to Yourself in Your very presence.

Gone in a Flash

*Your thunder was heard in the whirlwind, your lightning
lit up the world; the earth trembled and quaked.*

PSALM 77:18 NIV

There's a rule in my house: be aware when you open the front or
back door, especially when a kid or a cat is around. We don't want
to lose anybody, human or animal. We live on a busy street, so our
motto is Safety First.

In other words, we always keep in mind that a young child
or frisky pet can dart past us into the big world beyond our home.
Once they're gone, it's sometimes hard to get them to come back
inside. A little prevention in advance is worth the peace of mind it
brings. It's our responsibility to protect the vulnerable members of
our family, and that includes feline and canine friends, too.

Frodo, our silver tabby, likes routine and stability. One day, a
summer thunderstorm hit the area. The booming thunder outside
spooked him badly. Somebody opened the front door to see how
bad the rain was.

This was the last we saw of our baby for three hours. Our
escape artist dashed around the side of the house and took refuge
under a long, low porch. We were lucky we had a general idea of
where he was so we could coax him back.

Lord, You are with us in quiet times but also when the
storms come. Help us to be good caregivers. We ask Your
protection over the animals You have entrusted to us.

Jak's Work

The heart of man plans his way,
but the LORD establishes his steps.
PROVERBS 16:9 ESV

Our black mini-cougar and agile hunter, Jak, was taking his usual nap on the black office chair. I nearly sat on him before noticing him, but then I perched on the front edge of the chair. I caught up on e-mail then stood up to get some files from the closet. As I turned back toward my desk, I stepped on something horrifyingly wet and squishy. My leg reflexed upward, but the unidentifiable matter was stuck to the bottom of my bare foot. Gaining my composure to look at it, I immediately recoiled. It seemed to be a regurgitated mouse.

"Dexter! I need to get in the bathroom!" I called to my son, pulling the squish off one foot with a tissue as I hopped down the hall on the other foot to begin cleanup.

Sometimes the hard work we do just isn't appreciated quite as we had hoped. Things become. . .upset. They don't go as planned. Jak understands. So do I.

Father God, thank You that even in the mishaps of life,
sometimes with crazy real-life metaphors brought to me
by my cat, You somehow still work in and through it all.

Sammy's Consoling Hug

When anxiety was great within me,
your consolation brought me joy.
PSALM 94:19 NIV

Two thousand miles from home, I sat on the sofa in my new
apartment. I tossed another tear-filled tissue into the small pile and
reached for a dry one. The stubborn tears would not relent their
streaming as loneliness closed in on me.

My tuxedo cat, Sammy, hopped up on the cushion next to me.
He'd been my best friend for six years and stood by me through
many storms in my life. He squeezed his little pads around my
fingers as if trying to hold my hand.

I blinked away my tears to look at him.

A comforting gaze flowed from his sweet amber eyes that
seemed to say, "Everything will be all right. God is with us." He took
gentle steps into my lap and raised his head to bump against my
forehead. Then he wrapped his paws around my neck and hugged
me. Tender treading kneaded my taut shoulders.

I hugged him back. While holding him against my chest, the
flood of tears diminished to a trickle.

Sammy pulled his paws from around my neck, curled up in my
lap, and purred.

"Yes, Sammy," I said as I stroked his sleek back. "Everything
will be all right."

I pushed back against the gloom of loneliness and found
comfort in remembering God is in our midst.

Heavenly Father, You blessed me with a feline
friend who knew well the art of consolation.

Training for Stardom

For physical training is of some value, but godliness
has value for all things, holding promise for both
the present life and the life to come.

1 TIMOTHY 4:8 NIV

Peanut, a seal point Himalayan, was "discovered" in an animal
shelter by Angie, who trains animals for roles in movies and
commercials. It wasn't long before Angie learned that Peanut could
not only perform certain simple tasks but she could also learn and
do complex patterns—a series of sequential actions. In one particular
movie scene, Peanut had to circle a playpen, then jump and stretch
out her hind legs so she could reach a latch and unfasten it. The last
part of the task was to run from what she'd done.

Angie says one secret for teaching cats is to take time with
them. Since food is a feline's priority, that's what she uses for
rewards during training. In the book *Animal Stars* other trainers
make some additional recommendations. Consistency, patience,
kindness, and early training are all keys to success and stardom.
Many of these animal trainers keep and enjoy these movie stars as
family members.

We, too, must be trained in the good things of God to
"perform" well. We're to give ourselves to the study of God's Word
where we receive "training in righteousness" (2 Timothy 3:16). The
reward? "Those who lead many to righteousness [will shine] like the
stars" (Daniel 12:3).

Lord, continue to teach me righteousness.

A Token of Esteem

For the wages of sin is death, but the gift of
God is eternal life in Christ Jesus our Lord.
ROMANS 6:23 NIV

Two days ago, I received a very special gift. Black Purrl gave me *most* of a wolf spider. I tried to be grateful: I really did. I managed not to scream or jump when she dropped it onto my bare foot. She had given me some of her precious game, and I needed to express proper appreciation. I praised her generosity and scratched her ears. I didn't dispose of the gift until she had left the room.

It's not the first time I've had my gratefulness challenged.

When I was a child, my mother insisted that I thank my relatives for each gift I received. The sweater that was two sizes too small? I said thanks. The picture book three years below my reading level? I said thank you. The ugly pink comb and brush? I wrote a gracious note. . .under duress. As an adult, I can appreciate that the giving of thanks is not for the gift, but for the love behind the gift.

An attitude of thanks focuses my attention on what is really important about gifts—the person who gives them.

Jesus Christ gave us the greatest gift ever when He gave Himself on the cross. Let us give thanks.

Dear Jesus, thank You for giving Your life for
us and for conquering death in our stead.
Thank You for the gift of eternal life.

Drawing Near

*"Turn to me and be saved, all you ends of
the earth; for I am God, and there is no other."*
Isaiah 45:22 NIV

Tinker just showed up on my parents' porch one day. They lived waaaaay out in the country. Lots of feral cats could be spotted in the woods near their home, but rarely did these animals approach the house. But Tinker. . . Tinker was different. He was either someone's lost pet, or he was just tired of the rugged fend-for-yourself lifestyle.

Mom and Dad tried to find his owner, but no one claimed him. He wasn't wearing a collar or a tag. After a couple of weeks of caring for Tinker, they decided to take him to the vet, get him some shots, and make him their own. Before long, Tinker had his own bed on the porch, a set of matching bowls, and a scratching post.

Like those feral cats, many of us wander aimlessly, finding sustenance where we can, fending for ourselves and hoping for the best. Oh, if we'd only draw near to our Father! He longs to take care of us. He longs to meet our needs. He longs to draw us in and make us members of His family.

Dear Father, remind me to draw close to You today.
I'm tired of trying to fend for myself. I need You to
nourish me, care for me, and wrap me in Your love.

Parable: The Ostrich and the Cat

God did not endow her [the ostrich] with
wisdom or give her a share of good sense.

JOB 39:17 NIV

Septuagenarian Gary learned one stormy night that, unlike the ostrich, his cat, Mittens, has more than her "share of good sense." Gary and his wife had been sleeping soundly when Mittens started jumping up on their bed after midnight. She never does this—nor had she ever stared into Gary's sleep-heavy eyes after pouncing. He finally reached out to pet her reassuringly in the storm. He found Mittens soaking wet.

What . . . ?

Gary got out of bed to make sure Mittens' kittens were all right. He stepped into water up to his knees—in the bedroom. Mittens had already moved her kittens to safety. Now she was trying to get Gary and his wife to move to safety. After the flood, their house had to be torn down and rebuilt, but everyone—including Mittens and her litter—came out without a scratch.

Job said, " 'Ask the animals, and they will teach you' " (Job 12:7). God endows His creatures with senses (or sense) that so often exceed pure instinct. Job goes on to say that birds can tell us things and fish can give us information (Job 12:7–8). None of this should surprise us since Jesus said that even stones would praise Him, given the opportunity (see Luke 19:40).

All praise to You, Creator God! There is none like You!

Mouse in the House

"With my great power and outstretched arm I made the earth and its people and the animals that are on it, and I give it to anyone I please."
JEREMIAH 27:5 NIV

I looked up from my easy chair in the living room and came face-to-face with a mouse. He was the cutest little thing. Brown and sleek, he scampered across the carpet in my direction. My first thought was to lift my open-toed slippers into the air so he wouldn't run across them.

He saw me and stopped cold, rising on his back legs to stare me down. Then he zipped back to the kitchen where I believe his entry point into the house was located.

"I need a cat," I told my sister on the phone. She jokingly offered her Petey, the American shorthair that she'd had for five years.

"He can catch anything that moves," she said.

"Thanks, but I'm putting traps out. I don't want your baby getting caught in one," I told her. Well, the traps didn't work. I saw the mouse again a week later, bouncing down my steps from upstairs. I figured the rodent was attracted to a dripping faucet in my tub. I had to get that fixed, and I had to fix my pest problem, too.

My sister went on vacation two weeks later. I babysat her cat. Problem solved.

Lord, You created all animals for a purpose. We honor Your wisdom and foresight in giving us animal helpers.

A Willing Participant

*And we also thank God continually because, when you
received the word of God, which you heard from us,
you accepted it not as a human word, but as it actually is,
the word of God, which is indeed at work in you who believe.*

1 THESSALONIANS 2:13 NIV

My cousin Tracey's cat, Samantha, a long-haired Siamese, willingly participated in tea parties and dress up. While most animals will simply endure the many things a small child wants to do with them, she seemed to enjoy it. It seemed like she lived to be a part of whatever Tracey wanted to do. She listened to Tracey talk and seemed to understand what she said.

It was not unusual when we played with dolls for Tracey to have a "live" baby. Samantha wore dresses, bonnets, and bows and willingly posed like a princess as Tracey set her on display. She enjoyed the attention. When it was time for an outing, she happily let Tracey put her in the doll stroller for a walk around the neighborhood.

God is at work in our lives, but we aren't always willing participants. Unlike Samantha, I've been guilty of complaining about where God sent me or what He wanted me to do. I wasn't always a good listener and sometimes even resisted His plans. What about you?

Heavenly Father, help me to be excited about the things
You've asked me to do. Remind me of Your goodness
and love. Forgive me when I complain.

Nurse Pixie

The LORD sustains them on their sickbed
and restores them from their bed of illness.
PSALM 41:3 NIV

One day our tabby, Pixie, took a surprising interest in my husband. In the ten years since we had brought her home as a kitten, she had only aloofly tolerated him.

One evening, she joined him on the couch during a televised football game. The next day, she curled up with him in his chair while he read the newspaper. Day after day, if he sat still, Pixie was either in his lap or next to him. Although puzzled, he accepted her affection. . .not that he had a choice.

Soon after she adopted this bizarre behavior, my husband was diagnosed with stage-four cancer. Following his surgery, she took a greater interest in his care. Demanding that he go to bed when she deemed he'd been up too long, she snuggled against the area of his incision and purred with all her might. She altered her position to cover the other areas where the cancer had spread and gave him a round of maximum-effort purrs.

Did she sense the cancer developing before the symptoms appeared? We may speculate about our own little "cat scan," but Pixie's therapy method has lightened the weight of our arduous journey. The doctors are pleased with my husband's healing progress.

O loving God, we know You are beside us every step
of the way and delight in the furry little nurse You
sent to bring us cheer at this difficult time.

Focus

Brethren, I do not count myself to have apprehended; but one thing I do, forgetting those things which are behind and reaching forward to those things which are ahead, I press toward the goal for the prize of the upward call of God in Christ Jesus.
PHILIPPIANS 3:13–14 NKJV

I sat on the porch sipping my morning coffee, eyes barely cracked open, looking straight ahead. A soft breeze fluttered the leaves on the two poplars not far from the house while a family of robins chirped nearby. Jak, our jet-black cat, walked around in the yard and became very still. There was nothing unusual, at least from my eyes' half-opened view. Jolting me fully awake, Jak launched six feet in the air directly in my line of vision. I wondered if I really saw what I thought I saw, and then I saw the butterfly barely escaping death by the cat's clutches. Bright and high on adrenaline, the monarch flitted thankfully away, higher into the air. Jak stood still once more, this time a bit dejected, but only for a short time. He focused again on the hunt, not giving up.

Lord, thank You for fun surprises and encouraging moments from Your creation. Help me to press on in the life You have for me today with perseverance and hope, like Jak.

Contributor Index

Dee Aspin, a freelance writer, worked as a hospital RN and volunteered with Juvenile Justice Chaplaincy and Christian Singles' groups for three decades in her native California. She authored *Lord of the Ringless* and is now married. Dee has written for CBN, *Guideposts*, *Revel*, and more. Visit Dee at www.DeeAspin.com. Her readings can be found on pages 43, 140, 154, 165, and 171.

Renae Brumbaugh lives in Texas with two noisy children and two dogs. She's authored four books in Barbour's Camp Club Girls series. Her readings can be found on pages 25, 31, 36, 47, 55, 61, 66, 77, 88, 102, 107, 119, 128, 134, 141, 156, 163, 166, 172, and 181.

Katherine Douglas has authored numerous articles and books, as well as contributed to several anthologies. She enjoys leading women's Bible studies at her church. Kathy and her husband live in Fulton County, Ohio. Her readings can be found on pages 13, 24, 30, 37, 44, 54, 65, 75, 82, 87, 96, 103, 106, 115, 118, 126, 133, 138, 148, 153, 162, 170, 175, 179, and 182.

Award-winning author and speaker **Darlene Franklin** recently returned to cowboy country—Oklahoma. Darlene loves music, needlework, reading, and reality TV. Talia, a lynx point Siamese cat, proudly claims Darlene as her person. Darlene has published several titles with Barbour Publishing. Her readings can be found on pages 135, 144, 150, 158, and 168.

Shanna D. Gregor is a freelance writer, editor, and product developer who has served with various ministries and publishers. The mother of two young men, Shanna and her husband reside in Tucson, Arizona. Her readings can be found on pages 9, 16, 21, 28, 40, 50, 57, 63, 71, 80, 84, 90, 93, 99, 111, 122, 143, 160, 174, and 184.

Glenn A. Hascall is an accomplished writer with credits in more than fifty books. His articles have appeared in numerous publications, including the *Wall Street Journal*. His readings can be found on pages 14, 26, 139, 155, and 164.

Ardythe Kolb writes articles and devotions for various publications and is currently working on her third book. She serves on the advisory board of a writers' network and edits their newsletter. Her readings can be found on pages 8, 18, 34, 52, 70, 91, 109, 124, 145, and 159.

Shelley R. Lee is the author of *Before I Knew You*, *Mat Madness*, numerous magazine and newspaper articles, contributor to the *Daily Wisdom for Women 2014 Devotional Collection*, and several other Barbour projects. She resides in northwest Ohio with her husband of twenty-nine years, David, and their four grown sons. Her readings can be found on pages 11, 15, 23, 32, 38, 49, 58, 69, 74, 83, 89, 97, 101, 108, 113, 117, 125, 131, 136, 146, 149, 157, 167, 177, and 186.

Widely published author **Connie L. Peters** writes adult and children's fiction, creative and inspirational nonfiction, and poetry from Cortez, CO, where she and her husband host two adults with developmental disabilities. Her readings can be found on pages 10, 19, 29, 41, 53, 64, 72, 81, 94, 100, 112, 121, 130, 142, and 151.

Rachel Quillin is the author of several gift books and coauthor of the devotional prayer book *Prayers & Promises for Mothers*. She makes her home on a dairy farm in Stonecreek, Ohio, with her husband and children. Her readings can be found on pages 7, 17, 27, 33, 39, 45, 51, 56, 62, 68, 73, 79, 85, 92, 98, 104, 110, 116, 123, and 129.

Janet Ramsdell Rockey is a freelance Christian writer living in Tampa, Florida, with her Realtor husband and their two cats. She has written other works for Barbour Publishing, including her 180-day devotional, *Discovering God in Everyday Moments*. Her readings can be found on pages 12, 22, 173, 178, and 185.

Paula Swan is an artist and teacher from Toledo, Ohio, where she lives with her husband of eighteen years and their five pets. Her first publication was at the age of six; Paula attributes her love of words to the influence of her grandfather, Chester Arthur Smith, who taught her to read. She shares his passion for fairy tales and legends. She is an active member of Holland Free Methodist Church. Her readings can be found on pages 46, 60, 76, 127, and 180.

Cheryl Elaine Williams, resident of Pittsburgh, PA, is involved with family and church activities, gardening, and crafting for craft shows. She recently took two rescue animals into her house. She's published in sweet teen Young Adult fiction and in *Chicken Soup*-type anthologies, including Barbour Books' *Heavenly Humor for the Cat Lover's Soul*. Her readings can be found on pages 20, 35, 42, 48, 59, 67, 78, 86, 95, 105, 114, 120, 132, 137, 147, 152, 161, 169, 176, and 183.

Scripture Index